STRANGER
IN
MY BED

STRANGER IN MY BED

by

Beverly Slater

WITH

Frances Spatz Leighton

illustrated with photographs

ARBOR HOUSE

NEW YORK

Library of Congress Cataloging in Publication Data

Slater, Beverly.
    Stranger in my bed.   3 7 e 0 0 1 1

    1. Amnesia—Patients—Biography. 2. Slater,
Beverly. I. Leighton, Frances Spatz. II. Title.
RC394.A5S43 1984   362.1'9685232 [B]   84-2930
ISBN 0-87795-594-8

Manufactured in the United States of America

10 9 8 7 6 5 4 3 2 1

This book is dedicated to those beloved strangers who call themselves my family: my parents, Harry and Ann; the little people who call me "Granny," Aryn and Perri; my husband, Harold; and my children, Joanie and Stuart . . . And it is also dedicated to Hugh Carter, who changed my life . . .

—BEVERLY SLATER

Acknowledgments

There is a special place in my heart for all the people who helped me research and fit together the pieces of my life when I was that other, earlier Beverly as well as helping me understand the Beverly Slater that I am today: Steve Weisman, Mari Slater, Shirley Wolf, Stan Wolf, Erma Wolf, Bob Wolf, Evelyn Portnoy, Bernice Herlick, Paul Slater, Dr. Michael O'Connor, Dr. Raymond LaFlare, Dr. Elliot Atkins, Elaine Garfinkle, Marvin Garfinkle, Dr. Raymond Veeder, Lucile Slater, Ken Hoyt, Renée Fellman, Rosalyn Teplick, Fayne Garber, Lennie Garber, Ruth Goldstein, Marty Goldstein . . . and to the woman I enjoyed working with so much, my editor, Eleanor Johnson.

Contents

IV

SEARCH FOR A PAST—A DETECTIVE STORY

V

HITTING BOTTOM

VI

TO LIVE AGAIN

VII

REACHING OUT

Something had killed me, and yet I was alive. But I was alive without a memory, without a name. . . . I was buried alive in a void . . .

—HENRY MILLER
Tropic of Capricorn

An Opening Note

"I saw Mrs. Slater this afternoon for an hour in an attempt to elucidate whether her current condition had any neurological basis, whether it was entirely hysterical, or whether it was a combination of the two. My session with her in the morning did not lead me to believe that she was simulating amnesia . . ."

—RAYMOND VEEDER, M.D./dh
Director of Consultation and Community Services

I

WAKING UP

1

Do You Know Who You Are?

*H*al and I were on our way back from vacation—the same vacation that we had started three years before, just when the terrible thing happened that crashlanded my life and the lives of everyone in my family. At 7 A.M. we were almost the only ones in the airport. One other couple, very well dressed, finally came over and sat down beside us. After the first hellos, Hal and the woman wandered off to look at a sign.

The man smiled at me. "I'm Carter."

I smiled back. "I'm Slater."

"*Carter* of *Plains.*"

"*Slater* of *Philadelphia.*"

"Plains, as in peanuts." He was looking at me expectantly.

"Philadelphia," I replied, "as in scrapple." What was going on here?

He seemed determined to get a message across and I hadn't the slightest idea why. "I don't believe you understood," he said, leaning forward. "I am *Hugh* Carter—Senator Carter—of Plains, *Georgia.*"

Now I realized what was wrong. He must be waiting for *my* first name. "I'm *Beverly* Slater of Philadelphia, *Pennsylvania.*"

He tried again, "My cousin is *Jimmy* Carter."

So *that* was it—he wanted to compare families! I didn't know which of my cousins to mention. "My *husband* is *Harold* Slater." What an asinine conversation! But I decided to humor him.

He looked shocked. "My God, doesn't the name *Jimmy Carter* mean anything to you?"

Well, two could play at this game. "Doesn't the name *Harold Slater* mean anything to you?"

"Oh, my God," he said, "I'm talking about *President* Carter."

"Oh." *Now* it was making sense. "Of what company?" I was hoping it was something I would recognize, like AT&T, or Arnold Bread.

He shook his head. "Of the United States. He was the president of the United States. Doesn't that mean anything to you? Where have you been?"

By this time, Harold and the woman had returned and caught the end of our conversation. "Don't be hurt," Harold said. "She's not trying to put you down. She's had amnesia."

"Oh, my God," said Senator Carter. "This gives me the strangest feeling I've ever had."

"You ought to try the feeling on the *other* side," I said, "if you want to know what strange is . . ."

I woke up to a world of hazy white. Strangers stood around my bed, their mouths opening and closing, making sounds that had no meaning.

I closed my eyes.

"Beverly, are you awake? Oh, nurse, I think she's awake." The voices. Every time I opened my eyes there were the voices. "Nurse, I think she's coming to."

I felt the pain in my head, my throat. I tried to pull the tubes out but something was restraining my hand. I wanted to touch the pain, wipe it away.

Questions. Always questions. "Beverly Slater, do you know where you are? Beverly, do you know who you are? Nod your head if you do." I closed my eyes. I didn't know what everyone wanted. Why wouldn't they leave me alone?

If I slept, I could hide from them. But I kept opening my eyes. "Beverly, are you awake?" "Beverly, do you know who you are?" "No, you mustn't try to pull the tubes out. No, no."

"Do you know who this is?" "Do you recognize what I'm holding? Nod your head if you do."

I did not nod.

I wished they would shut up.

Slowly the blurry faces came into focus, but I still didn't understand the noises they were making. I would look at these mouths taking different shapes as they opened and closed—overlapping faces moved forward and backward, fading in and out. Disjointed conversations around me. *Strangers* peering at me. Everyone was a stranger.

But there was one voice I was getting used to. "Hi, hon, how are you? You're looking better. Do you know who I am? I'm your husband. I'm Harold, and I'm with you. You're going to be all right."

What was "all right"?

"You know who is here to see you? Your mother and your dad. Everybody's here."

I had no idea what he meant.

Time seemed endless, the questions seemed endless . . . "What is your name?" "Do you recognize me?" "Nod your head if you understand me—do you understand me?"

I refused to nod for these silly fools. I couldn't talk with all the tubes in my nose and throat anyway. I didn't know who they were and I didn't care. For that matter, I didn't know who *I* was and I didn't care. Why did they keep bothering me?

One day a doctor took a tube out of my throat. "I think we'll see if she can get along without the respirator." I was so glad to have it out and I tried to talk, but all that came out were gutteral sounds. Soon I was gasping for breath and the doctor was forcing the respirator back down my throat. I tried to stop him. I didn't want that pain again. The doctor won.

In a few days the respirator was removed again and this time it stayed out.

Now I could talk. At first it was only gibberish, but then suddenly I could say a few words that people did understand. I liked seeing their amazement. "She's coming around," said the doctors. "She understands. That's great. Do you know where you are?"

"No," I croaked. "Am I supposed to?"

"You're in the hospital. You're going to be all right."

There were those words *all right* again. I still didn't know what they meant.

"Do you know where you live?"

"No. Am I supposed to?"

A nurse was leaning over me. "Hello, what's your name?"

"I don't know, what's *your* name?"

"I'm Nurse Louise. Now tell me your name."

"Go to hell."

One person had the right idea. He always came in booming, "Hi, Beverly Slater. *You* are Beverly Slater and I am Dr. O'Connor. How is Beverly Slater today?"

I liked him. He didn't make me try to remember who I was—he *told* me. And if he thought I was Beverly Slater, well, that was good enough for me—especially since it seemed to make him happy.

Beverlyslater, Beverlyslater. At first I thought it was all one word. I would say it in a rush, "Beverlyslater."

But the man called Harold confused me—he kept calling me Beverly. If I was Beverlyslater, why was he calling me Beverly?

And he was calling me other things that made no sense at all— "honey," "darling," "sweetheart." Who were *they*? Who was he? Not that I cared particularly. I kept wishing he wouldn't hang around so much. Whenever I opened my eyes he'd be there, looking at me, talking at me, telling me he loved me.

Everyone was saying that. "We love you." "I love you." "We *all* love you." Who cared? What was love? I hadn't the foggiest.

At first it was fun showing off that I could speak, even if none of it made much sense. But eventually the game palled. I became tired of the same old questions.

"What's your name?"

"Do you know who I am?"

"Where do you live?"

Did I know what this or that was? And if I did give the right name, they would ask what it was for. They showed me a clock. I could point out the numbers on it—"That's a two and that's a four and that's twelve."

"What do you call it?"

"I don't know."

"Do you know what time it is?"

"What's time?"

"Can you tell time with a clock?"

"What? What do you mean?"

They explained it to me, and I relearned it very quickly.

What did I know? What could I do? That's what the doctors wanted to know.

I could speak. I could read words—but I still had to keep asking what so many things meant. At least I knew how to ask a question and sometimes I even understood their explanation. But why did they have to speak so fast?

I started to remember faces but I still couldn't remember names—sometimes not even my own.

"Hi, babe, I'm here again. I'm Harold, your husband. Do you remember me now?"

I just looked at him. "I'm Harold," he repeated. "What's your name?"

"I'm Harold," I rasped.

"No," he said. "*You're* Beverly. I'm Harold. You're my wife, Beverly. Say it. Beverly. Say it—Beverly."

I didn't want to say it. "I don't know you," I lashed out. "Shit, shit, shit. Bitch, get out."

I could see that he was shocked. It pleased me. He left. But he came back the next day. Sometimes I was happy and eager to listen to him and other times I was irritable and shouted curses.

When I was happy and did not curse, Harold called me a good girl and when I went into a tantrum and cursed, he said I was a bad girl. When I was a good girl, he sat and stroked my hair and kissed my cheek before he left. When I was a bad girl, he just got up and left.

So now I thought I knew how to get rid of all those people standing around my bed, looking at me sadly or with forced smiles. I would just throw tantrums.

I swore at all those smiling faces—the doctors, the nurses, the relatives—everyone who kept assuring me of his or her love.

"Goddamn son of a bitch," I said. "Fuck you. Shut up."

Harold apologized to a nurse for my language and she laughed, saying that cursing was not at all uncommon for head injury patients, often such patients behave in a manner exactly opposite to their normal selves. A nun had awakened from a concussion screaming obscenities.

"Your wife will get over it, Mr. Slater."

Harold said he had *never* heard me swear like this and was tremendously relieved that it wouldn't last forever.

Sometimes the doctors laughed. Sometimes they said, "There, there. That's not nice, is it?"

"Damn bastard."

Relatives did not react so mildly. They looked hurt, stricken. I was glad. Maybe now they would stay away and quit tormenting me with all those questions. "Do you remember this? Do you remember that?"

"Get out, get out, get out, son of a bitch."

"Better let her cool down," a nurse would say. "Perhaps she shouldn't have this much company."

But no matter what I did, the man they called Harold kept coming back. Why?

With the I.V. out of my arm, I was now feeding myself. I picked up food with my fingers, stuffed it into my mouth. The nurses urged me to take more. I didn't know why I should bother pleasing them but sometimes I'd oblige anyway.

One day a nurse brought in the tray with something particularly ugly on it—long, long strands of things intertwined. "What is this shit?" I demanded, lifting up a handful.

"It's called spaghetti," the nurse said, wiping my hand and handing me a fork. I threw the spaghetti on the floor.

"Who the hell are you?" I roared at the stranger who had just come in.

"Mother, I'm your child. I'm Joanie. Don't you recognize me?"

Hateful creature. She was fiddling in her purse, pulling something out. She showed me a picture. "Pretty girl," I said. "Who is that?"

"Mother, that's me."

She burst into tears and ran out of the room.

"Go to hell, bitch," I yelled after her.

Now the other one was coming in. "Get the hell out, miss," I hissed.

"Now, now, Beverly. I'm your husband. I'm Harold, remember?"

"Who the shit cares. Get out, get out, get out."

He just stood there looking at me. "I'll get the nurse." He came in with a nurse and doctor. "I think she's getting overexcited. My daughter is very upset—"

"Shut up, shut up, shut up." I wanted to drown out his voice.

"—and I think maybe we'd better not let any more visitors come for a few days. It just makes her like this."

I wanted to hit him. "Shut up, shut up, shut up."

"There, there," said Dr. O'Connor, patting my hand, smiling at me. I calmed down and smiled back. "That's a good idea," he said. "For a time it might be better if she sees just you and gets used to you."

In a way, I understood. They were going to do something about those people and if Dr. O'Connor said so, it was all right.

"Shit, shit, shit," I rasped. I didn't want Dr. O'Connor to stop paying attention to me.

"Now, Beverly Slater," he said, "now, now. Quiet down."

Somehow the one they called my son, Stuart, didn't annoy me as much as Joanie did.

The face that became most familiar to me was Harold's. He came all the time. Every day. Some times several times a day. Sometimes I called him "sir," sometimes "miss." I didn't know him. I didn't like him.

He kept trying to explain things to me. "I'm your husband and I love you, so I come to see how you are."

"I'm okay, how are you?"

"A lot better now that you're talking. I brought you something— a lovely nightgown. You have more in your house."

That was truly where everything nice was. "I want to go house."

"No, dear, say, 'I want to go *home*.' Your *home* is your *house*."

"I don't understand."

"Well, it's not easy to explain. Your home could be just a trailer or an apartment in a big building, but it's still *home*. *You* live in a *house*. That's home to you."

I had no idea what he was talking about. I tuned him out.

When he'd finished I tried again. "Are you taking me house?"

"Not today, dear. Not for a while."

"Okay." I was distracted—Dr. O'Connor was coming in, beaming at me. "How's Beverly Slater today?"

I didn't curse. I gave him my best smile as he touched my wrist, looked into my eyes, examined the back of my head. He was so gentle and cheerful I wished I could follow him out of the room. I watched him as he walked over to the nurses' station.

Then Harold left the room to talk to him. I felt as though I'd been a good little girl.

Once I had cut down on my cursing and cleaned up my act a bit, Harold let the children visit me again. He did his best to make Joanie's reentry into my life a little smoother.

The idea was to make me curious to see this newcomer. Stepping out into the hall, he said, "Oh, look who is here to see Beverly. I'm so glad to see you. Beverly will be, too." In the few days since I'd last seen anyone in my family aside from Harold, he had mentioned many times that I had a daughter named Joanie whom I was going to like very much. Now, when he brought her in, she seemed so friendly, putting her arms around me. I decided I liked her. Especially since she brought me a present. So, we were over the first hurdle.

Harold had warned Joanie not to ask me questions I couldn't answer—he'd learned from experience that nothing infuriated me more—and she was nervously bringing up safe subjects. She mentioned that she had to get a dress fixed because she was going to a party. "There's a dressmaker upstairs in Haddonfield," I said.

Harold looked stunned. "Where in Haddonfield?"

"Kings Highway and Haddon Avenue."

Harold rushed out to get a nurse and told me to tell her what I had just said.

"I don't know," I said. I really didn't. I couldn't remember, and when they told me the address it still didn't jog my memory. "I don't know," I said. They dropped it, but I could tell that this had made them excited and hopeful.

In the second week, with the tubes out, I had become ambulatory and soon I was here, there and everywhere, exploring this wonderful, magical new world. Bells rang, walls opened. People appeared and disappeared.

One day a wall opened and I walked in. A door closed and I was caged in a box. Suddenly it moved. I was shocked. The door opened. I ran out, bumping into people. Finally I was found and returned to my floor. A nurse showed me the elevator door and said, "No, no. Beverly, don't get on the elevator. It's a no-no unless we are with you. Do you understand?"

"Go to hell," I croaked. "Shit, shit, shit."

Her solution was to put a sign on the back of my hospital gown: "RETURN TO INTENSIVE CARE, NEUROSURGERY, 3rd FLOOR."

One day I wandered into the cafeteria, drawn by the sight of so many people. For a time I stood in the line with them, just staring at their faces, listening to them talk, and then I wandered off to a brightly lighted place where rows and rows of pretty foods were sitting in a long shiny box. I walked up and down, putting my fingers into the various dishes. I found a pretty red cherry in one of them and popped it into my mouth.

I was having so much fun I didn't even notice that a crowd of people had gathered around me, all talking excitedly. "Where does she belong?" "Who is she?" Someone read the sign on my back, "RETURN TO INTENSIVE CARE, NEUROSURGERY, 3rd FLOOR." Gently, a doctor introduced himself and led me back to my ward.

I prattled happily all the way back. Finally we were standing by my bed. "Good-bye, Beverly," he said.

"Are you taking me home today?"

I had an obsession about going home.

"No, Beverly."

"Go to hell, you bastard."

I was angry—he had betrayed me. I had walked with him like a good girl and he wouldn't take me where I wanted to go—wherever that was.

"Beverly Slater talked about having absolutely no memory from anything that happened prior to her finding herself in the hospital and I was impressed with the fact that this was not the kind of amnesia that I, personally, had ever seen before since it was not a matter of not knowing who she was, not recognizing people or places and having absolutely no memory of what had gone before. Mrs. Slater described her amnesia as though she were a newborn babe who knew nothing about anything and had to be taught about the smallest details of everyday living."*

---

*This and all other italicized comments at the end of alternate chapters were written by Raymond Veeder, M.D., who treated and evaluated Beverly Slater.

2

Breaking Out

*G*radually, Harold helped me to understand that we had been preparing for a vacation on an island called Jamaica when I had had an accident, and that was why I was in the hospital. The vacation was going to be fun. It was going to be an adventure.

There were so many words to explain—*vacation, accident, hospital, adventure.* A car had struck me. That was a big thing and it moved fast. He held his hands out to show me how big and he brought them together—slap—to show me how the car had hit me.

But I was going to be all right and some day he would still take me to Jamaica because that had been my big wish. But first he was going to take me home, and that was also going to be an adventure. So I mustn't feel bad about being in the hospital, because very soon I would be leaving and I would start having adventures. At home.

When was he going to take me to Jamaica? Soon.

When was I going home? Soon.

But meanwhile I was having adventures right here in the hospital.

One day I noticed strange white mist floating past a window. It reminded me of the gauzy haze right after the accident.

"That's snow," a nurse said.

"Snow?"

"Yes, snow. Do you remember snow?"

"No. What do you do with it?"

"Nothing. Walk in it. Kick it around. Make snowballs and throw them at someone."

"Can I have one?"

"We'd have to ask the doctor. Snowballs are very cold and you wouldn't like them." *Cold* I understood. Cold was when you wanted another blanket. But this snow was so pretty. How could it be cold?

"Where do snowballs come from?"

"You mean snow. Snow falls from the sky and people make snowballs to play with."

Later, when Harold arrived, I was standing mesmerized, my elbows on the windowsill. Together we stood by the window as the frothing, swirling sea of white particles fell. I was fascinated by the way some of the flakes hit the window and turned to water.

"Where does the snow come from?"

"From the clouds. I'll get you a book." Aha . . . he had given me a different answer from that of the nurse. Whom was I supposed to believe? I often asked several people the same question just to see how their answers varied.

I was learning so many new words. Harold said we were a *couple,* he and I, and if you saw a man and woman together, they were a couple. One day as we watched a man and woman approaching, I said, "There's a nicely dressed couple."

"Beverly, they're your parents. Don't you recognize your mother and father yet?"

I looked closer. My mother took my hand and said, "Beverly, we've been here every day, every day they would let us see you. Don't you know us yet? I'm mother. This is father."

I just stared at them, refusing to speak. Why was everyone pressuring me all the time to remember? Father, mother. That must be their names. I was now calling everyone "miss." Then Harold corrected me and said somebody was a "sir," not a "miss," so for a while I called everyone—men and women—"sir." The nurses were "sir." Even Joanie was "sir." Harold said I was still wrong. I wished he would make up his mind.

Harold eventually got through to me about this father and mother business. It meant, he said, that they had *made* you.

"What do you mean?"

"You came out of your mother's body."

It was a hideous thought. I couldn't believe it. Me? Coming out of that little woman's body? But the worst was yet to come. Joanie had come out of *my* body. So had Stuart. It was scary. Spooky.

"I don't want to hear about it."

"All right, dear." He rocked me in his arms. "Don't worry about it. We'll talk about it some other time."

I tried to explain to Harold what had happened to me while I was unconscious. . .

Three times, maybe four, a gray-haired lady came to my bedside and, looking at me with kindly eyes, said, "You have to live or Pop Pop will die." One night she said, "I'm not coming back tomorrow because you are going to wake up."

And she didn't come again.

Days or maybe weeks later, when Harold told me how lucky it was that I hadn't died, I said, "Oh, I knew I wouldn't die because the lady told me so."

"What lady?"

"The nice lady."

"What did she look like?"

"She looked different. She had white hair."

"What did she say? How did you know you wouldn't die?"

"She said, 'You have to live or Pop Pop will die.' "

He looked very upset.

"Oh, God, did you know who she was talking about? Who is Pop Pop?"

"I don't know, but I liked her."

"What did she look like? What was she wearing?"

"I don't know, but it was pink. The same as the nurse. Pink."

"My God, she was buried in pink. Sweetheart, don't be alarmed, but that was my mother you're describing. But you must have been dreaming because she isn't here anymore. She passed away."

"I know she's not here. She said she wouldn't come anymore."

"But sweetheart, she can't come anymore. She's dead. I can't believe it. She was buried in a pink dress. You saw it, remember? No, I guess you can't remember. But you dreamed it. You remembered in your subconscious mind. I'll have to tell the doctors about this. A very important dream."

"It wasn't a dream. I saw her and she stayed with me and she said the same thing every time. What's Pop Pop?"

"Pop Pop is a person and he's too sick to come to see you now. He's my father, sweetheart. He was married to the lady you thought you saw. See, darling, mother just died and I guess she was telling you that he couldn't stand a second shock so soon. He's taking it very hard."

"What does that mean, taking it very hard?"

"He's very upset, very sad about her dying."

"He shouldn't be sad. It's very nice, dying."

Why was Harold crying? It was true—dying *was* very nice. In fact, I wasn't at all sure I was glad to be back. I thought about it often, how it had looked. The first time was in the ambulance. I found myself flying through a tunnel, and it was wonderful to be so light—like a feather, like a leaf, like a blade of grass. In the distance, I could see the most brilliant light and I wanted to get to it. I wanted to go. I could hardly wait to reach it. I felt so good. So carefree, so joyous. So lighter-than-air. I was swept on and on. But then suddenly something was pulling me back. I didn't want to go but somehow I knew I mustn't argue. I saw the number three. I let myself float back and then the light was gone and all I could feel was the pain.

Then it happened again. Everything was the same. The light, the wonderful feeling, again the number three. And again the pain. Later, Harold said I had had two cardiac arrests and both had been in ambulances—first going to the hospital and then, very soon after, when I was taken to another hospital for a CAT scan.

Harold asked me what the number three meant. I didn't know. I thought often about the number three. What did it mean? I liked reliving the experience of rushing through the tunnel to the light. For some reason, I had no trouble remembering that.

Love, love, love.

If love was attention, everyone loved me. I was the pet of the hospital. I was the freak in the zoo. Everyone came to look at me and marvel. Nurses from other floors came by for a peep, ushered in and out by my familiar nurse faces. Doctors from other hospitals stopped by to have a look, hear me speak.

Many were warned not to be shocked at my language. "She's rather spicy," I heard one doctor warn another. I asked what spicy meant. "Spicy things are good. Spicy food tastes good. It's tasty."

Suddenly I was scared. "Am I tasty?"

"I would say so," the doctor said.

Now I knew. They were going to eat me. The nurse was always bringing in a tray, saying, "Now eat this. It's tasty. Doesn't it look tasty?"

This was really scary stuff. I didn't like the taste of anything and I didn't want to look tasty.

I asked Harold if they were going to eat me.

"That's the dumbest thing I ever heard. Of course not. *Dumb!* Whatever gave you that idea?"

"I don't know." I was relieved—but only partially. Now there was a new description for me—dumb. Whatever that was. From the sound of Harold's voice, it was not a good thing to be.

More than ever, I was anxious to get out of the hospital. Dr. O'Connor said that I could go home when I was ready and could do things.

"What things?"

"We'll see."

Soon I found myself in a strange room where a kind lady asked all kinds of questions and played games with me. The big deal was to put a square peg into a square hole and a triangular peg into a triangular hole and a round peg into a round hole. The first day I failed dismally.

After three days I finally puzzled it out and then I was so amazed and delighted with my new game that I couldn't be stopped from playing it over and over again. Einstein could not have felt smarter. And I knew that every new thing I learned took me closer to going *home.* Skipping rope was evidently another skill I was expected to master before I could leave. That was harder than square pegs and round holes. But I got it!

Then I had to match words to pictures. It was so much fun learning what things looked like. My score may not have been high, but judging from the pictures, it looked like there was an exciting world out there—and it made me all the more anxious to get at the real thing.

I was aware that Harold and Dr. O'Connor had become friends, but all I cared about was going home.

"Can I go home now?"

"It's getting closer and closer."

According to Harold, Dr. O'Connor had said that when I felt fine and I was no longer in pain I could go home. So I decided to lie about how I felt. When Dr. O'Connor asked, I would say, "Fine," even though the back of my head—where I could feel the indentation—really hurt. I stopped telling him whenever I had a headache.

One day Harold said, "If you see yourself, maybe you'll remember who you are." He had a framed, shiny object in his hand. Joanie snatched it away from him.

"No, dad, no. Don't let her see herself with all those black-and-blue marks."

He quickly put the shiny object back in his briefcase.

Another day the nurse said, "Come, Beverly, you are going to have a shower."

From the sound of her voice, I knew this was going to be a wonderful new adventure. She led me into a white tiled room. There it was again—the long, shiny object, but bigger, and this time on the wall. I stood in front of it, not having the vaguest idea who the image before me was.

"This is you, Beverly," the nurse said. "Come see how you look." She helped me off with my robe. I was Eve in the Garden of Eden, seeing her reflection in a pond. I smiled. I laughed. This was me! I hardly noticed my face. But my body fascinated me.

"Let me see you," I said.

The nurse looked startled. "I haven't time," she said, suddenly brusque. "I have to get you washed."

It was probably the longest shower I would ever take. The water felt so good as it washed over me, so warm and kind. It even made me forget the pain in my head.

After I got out of the tub I insisted on standing in front of the mirror again.

I started to run my hands up and down my body. It felt good.

"Don't wear it out," the nurse said, laughing nervously. "You can have another shower tomorrow and see if you still look the same. You have a nice figure."

"I do? What's that?"

"A nice body. You are nice and slim."

"What's that?"

"Slim. That means you are not fat. I will show you someone fat some day and you will see the difference. Okay?"

"Okay." Whatever turned her on.

"Now put on this pretty pink robe from home. Okay?"

"Okay." Everything nice came from home.

In the fifth week, I graduated from intensive care to a private room with a television set. I was supposed to learn about the world from this noisy box, but I didn't like it and I couldn't understand the pictures that kept moving, moving—much too fast. I was far more impressed with water coming out of a faucet. If they had let me, I would have sat and watched it for hours.

I desperately wanted to be treated like a grown-up, and would resort to lying, if necessary, to convince people that I was one. Once someone brought me a book—a novel—not realizing I couldn't understand the words. I insisted—and indeed half-believed it myself—that I had read it in one day. Harold was totally unconvinced.

"I don't believe it. Are you telling the truth? Beverly, tell the truth."

I threw a tantrum.

"I *am* telling the truth."

"There, there," he said, "you did. You read a whole big book, didn't you?"

"Yes, I did. Yes, I did. I read very fast." I looked at the faces around me—the nurse, my family—and felt smug. They believed me. I had pulled it off.

Then there was the matter of the Eagles team. Harold and the doctors and the male friends who came to visit me talked endlessly about the merits of the various members of the Eagles. "The whole team came to see me," I said.

They looked at me. "Why were they here?"

"They invited me to the game."

"The Eagles?"

"Yes."

"What game?"

"The game you're talking about." Loud guffaws—but I didn't care. I would have said anything to seem a part of this adult world.

■ ■ ■

One day I decided it was Stuart's fault that I couldn't go home. "Miss, miss," I kept telling him, "can you help me get the fuck out of here?"

"I'm sorry, mom, I can't."

"You bastard, you're no good. Can't you get me out of here?"

"Where would you go?"

"I'm going home, you jerk. Don't you know anything, miss?"

"Where is home?"

"What do you care? Just get me out of here."

"Mom, please, you have to stay."

"Why do you call me that dumb name? My name is Beverlyslater."

Now he had tears in his eyes and I couldn't for the life of me figure out why. "But don't you remember my name is Slater, too? Oh, mother!"

"Mother, shit! Are you getting me out of here?"

"No."

"Then get the fuck out of here. I don't need you."

"Mom, mom, don't talk that way. You never talked that way."

"Shut up, you bastard, get out of my room."

Harold appeared.

Now I flew into a rage. "Who the hell are you? You're not telling me what to do. I'm getting out of here." Crying, I rushed for the door, but Harold grabbed me and led me back to bed. He rocked me in his arms until I stopped crying.

One day I ran and ran and he followed and finally, with the help of strangers, caught me in the lobby. I was kicking and screaming and yelling obscenities but he just picked me up like a sack of potatoes and hauled me back to my room.

There was no escaping him. But at least he had promised to take me home if I was a good girl. Maybe now was good-girl time.

I had to get out. Good things must be happening out there. Adventures. It was all a big conspiracy to keep me from having adventures. Everyone else could come and go but they wouldn't let me come and go. Harold, Joanie, Stuart, everybody kept telling me everything was great at home. I would be glad to see how nice things were at home. I had to get there and see for myself.

Joan brought me a wonderful, big, cuddly stuffed animal. "It's a panda to keep you company. It's a present from your granddaughter because they won't let her come to see you."

"Oh."

"She's at home waiting for you. You'll see her when you get home. She's not much bigger than the panda." Joanie was laughing.

"Does the panda live at home?"

"She did live at my home just for a few days and now she's going to live at your home."

I hugged the panda. How wonderful it was. And it came from *home.*

Steve—the fellow they called Joan's husband—came in. "How are you, mom? You're looking happy today. I guess you like your panda. What's its name?"

"Its name is Beverly."

"Oh. How original. But why don't you call it Bevie so when I speak to you the panda won't answer?" Why were he and Joan grinning at each other?"

"What's *original?*" I said. "What does that mean?"

"Oh, boy. *Original.* Golly, Joanie, I'm going to start carrying my Webster's. Original, mom, that means something is one of a kind, like you are. You're one of a kind and I love you." He was hugging me and I didn't really have room in my arms to hug him *and* my panda.

"We all love you, mom." More hugs.

Love! There they went again. Telling me they loved me. What was love? I didn't have time to bother with it.

Joanie left the room. Now was my chance . . .

I grabbed Steve's hand. "I'm going home." I lowered my voice so Joanie or Harold wouldn't hear if they came in.

"Mom, where is home?" he asked very seriously.

Ah, now I was getting somewhere. "I don't know, but I'm going."

"Well, mom, you have to have some money to get home."

Nobody had told me about money yet. "Give me some money." I held out my hand.

Steve reached in his pocket and pulled out some coins. "That's all the change I have," he said, putting them in my hand. There were three coins.

"Twenty-five, thirty-five, forty," I said. "Is that all?"

"That's all."

"I'll take it and get more someplace else." I was very disappointed. But what had come over Steve? He had run out of the room to get Joan. "Look, she can count!" he said excitedly. "She added a quarter and a dime and a nickel."

They were looking at me with amazement. Evidently I had done something very good. I smiled with pride. "Do you want me to do it again?"

For the moment, at least, I forgot about going home.

II

STRANGER IN MY BED

3

A Place Called Home

*G*oing home. I was going home.

I ran to the nurses' station to tell them. "I'm going home."

"Good," they said. "Come back and see us."

"Okay. When?"

"We'll let you know."

"Good."

I told every doctor I saw. "I'm going home."

"That's fine."

Dr. O'Connor and Harold were talking in low voices. "What did he tell you?" I asked Harold after the doctor left. "Was he talking about me?"

"Yes, I'll tell you later."

"No, tell me, tell me."

"He said to be gentle with you."

"What's gentle?"

"I'll explain later. And to be patient."

"You're going to be a patient?"

"No, it's a different kind of patient. He wants me to take it easy and be patient with you until you learn things."

"Okay."

Home. I was going home. And so was a nurse. That was part of the deal I'd made with Dr. O'Connor. I was to be a good girl and do everything she said. I was to listen and she would explain how to do things. She was not like a nurse in the hospital. She was a practical nurse. She was not as expensive.

I didn't care if she was expensive or not. But it was an interesting thought that I could buy a person.

I had seen cars from my hospital windows but now I was actually getting inside one. And it moved. What fun! Harold drove, pointing out things as we went along. What big buildings! What big green things!

"Trees," said Harold.

I had seen trees in magazines at the hospital, but this was different. And then there were the houses . . . Yes, I knew houses. I had seen pictures of houses, but these were different and I didn't even know why. There were so many kinds but they were still called houses.

"Our house looks something like that," Harold said, pointing at one. "We're very close now."

I don't know what I was expecting. I guess I thought my house would be like another hospital with lots of brick and glass, but it was brown wood and smaller than a hospital and had a fancy door. And there were big white things on each side of the door.

"Pillars," Harold said. "Those are pillars."

"Who lives there?"

"You do. We do. It's your house. You're home."

As he walked me through the rooms, I was silent. I saw nothing that aroused a memory. So this was *home?* Harold opened a door and I looked into a darkened little cubicle. "These are your clothes," he said. "Everything in this closet is yours and I keep my clothes in a different closet."

He showed me another room. "This is your kitchen. Anything you want to eat is here and if there's anything else you want, the nurse or I can get it. Just tell us."

He showed me a room that was down a half flight of stairs, "This is the family room, the room the kids used to use a lot."

I looked at the orange rug. "I like it. Oh, I like it."

"Yes, it's especially nice with a fire going in the fireplace." He pointed to it. "I'll light it right now for you. Would you like that?"

"I don't know."

"Well, a lot of people know you're coming home today so I'm expecting a lot of them to show up to welcome you home. A fire would be nice."

And it was. I felt a little lonely, a little lost away from the only place I knew—the hospital—and my friendly nurses and doctors.

"Are people going to come here?" I asked.

"Yes. Everyone you saw at the hospital."

"Oh."

"And some are going to bring you presents, I'm sure. And you are going to meet your little granddaughter who sent you her panda because she couldn't come visit you herself."

The panda was on the bed along with my suitcase. Harold unpacked my case as I sat on the bed watching. "What is this?" he asked sternly, suddenly pulling out my restraints. "Why did you take them?"

"I don't know." I could tell I had done something wrong.

"Well, I'm going to have to take them back. That's something you must remember. You do not take anything from someone's house when you go to visit unless they give it to you."

"Okay," I said. I could have told him why I had the restraints. I had hidden them so that the nurses could not put them on me again. The suitcase was a good hiding place. But I didn't say anything.

Suddenly a strange creature appeared in the doorway. I jumped up.

"Don't be scared," said Harold. "That's a cat. Don't you remember, I told you we had a cat and its name is Midnight—Night for short. That's supposed to be funny. See, the cat is all white, so the children called it Midnight because night is dark—black."

I wasn't laughing. I was thinking that the cat was something like my panda. "Why doesn't it stand up?"

"It is standing up. It is standing up on four legs." The cat had come over and was rubbing itself against my legs. I might not remember Midnight but Midnight remembered me. It was making a little noise. "Hello," I said, delighted. "How are you?"

Harold sighed. "God, give me strength. Beverly, for God's sake, don't you know a cat doesn't talk? People talk. Animals don't talk. Don't be a dummy. People will think you're a dummy if you talk like that to a cat."

"You're mad at me."

"No, honey, I'm just nervous. How would you know these things? I'm sorry. See, the cat wants you to pet it, like this. Animals don't talk. They just love and he's trying to love you."

Here we went with *love* again. Still, the cat's fur was soft and I liked petting this creature with its funny little noise.

"Can I play with it?"

"Of course."

Instantly, I was on the floor, trying to hug Midnight. But Midnight didn't want to be hugged, so I got on my hands and knees and tried to play his game, following him around and then lying on the floor in a ball.

When I looked up Harold was standing there, watching us, shaking his head. "You don't have to copy the cat. The cat is not impressed that you are trying to be like it. Just pet him like I showed you. That's what he wants."

My first visitors were Joanie and her children. I had never seen little people before. They were like my panda. "When did you get them?"

I could see that Joanie was trying not to cry. "This is Aryn— going on four. And this is baby Perri and she is six months old. You paced the hospital corridor when I was in labor with each of them, mother."

"Oh, aren't they cute?" I said. "Can I play with them?"

I didn't know what she was crying about. I was delighted to see these tiny people, and as for *labor* in the hospital, that was completely over my head.

But at first the children seemed to prefer Midnight, and I was a little jealous. I was used to being the center of attention. But since I was fascinated by the cat, too, I couldn't really blame them. And eventually they turned to me.

Aryn sat on the floor, so I sat on the floor. She showed me her doll, so I showed her my panda. Soon we were talking and laughing and throwing playing cards all over the living room. Joanie started to tell Aryn to stop but then she caught herself and said, "Whatever you and grandma want to do."

"Who is that?" Aryn asked me, pointing at my nurse.

"She is the nurse who takes care of me."

"My mommy takes care of me."

"The nurse is my mommy," I said.

"No, she isn't, Beverly," Harold said. "But she is a nice lady. You have another mommy. Remember?"

"Oh yes," I said, "the little lady."

"That's the one. She is the grandmother of Joanie and the great-grandmother of Aryn. Did you know that?"

"I don't care," I said. The subject bored me.

I was amazed by the baby Perri—she was not much bigger than Midnight and, she, too, walked on all fours. I asked Harold why one little person walked like me and one walked like a cat. He turned to Joanie and said, "You see what I'm up against?"

She looked at him sympathetically.

"I see. Mother, that's because she's only six months old. But when she gets as big as Aryn, she'll be walking just like us, too. In fact, sooner."

"Oh."

"I have an appointment to see a psychologist," Harold told Joanie, as though I weren't even there.

"An excellent idea, dad."

"I have to stay on an even keel," he continued. "It's hard to cope."

"What's a keel?" I asked.

"That's a boat," Harold said. "I'll show you a boat when we go to the shore at Atlantic City. It's part of a boat."

That sounded like fun.

"Oh, goody. I know what a boat is."

"Oh, goody," Harold echoed, with an edge of sarcasm.

"But mom's learning very fast and she's not a vegetable," Joanie said.

"Of course not," I said. "You eat vegetables. I know that."

They laughed. Others were arriving. The little couple who said they were my *parents*. And Shirley and Erma, who said they were my *friends*. And Stuart, who said he was my *son*, with a girl who said she was *his* friend and who looked to me as if she could be Joanie's twin.

After everyone had gone home, Harold took me out into the backyard. There was a rustling in the leaves of the tree. A cat scampered across the lawn and up a tree.

"A cat," I said.

"No," said Harold, "that's a squirrel. See the tail?"

I watched transfixed as the squirrel ran along a branch and twitched its tail. "Can I have it?" I asked.

"No, you have enough animal life around here. Anyway, it would be hard to catch."

"It would?" I was learning fast that nothing was easy—inside the hospital or out.

That night I went to sleep in the bed that Harold said was my own little bed, right next to his. He held my hand on top of the covers. It was strange having a stranger in my room—it hadn't been like that in the hospital.

"Do you want me to get in bed with you so you won't be alone?" he asked.

What a silly question . . . I wasn't alone. I had my panda. "No, thank you."

After Harold had gone to work the next day, the nurse took me with her into the kitchen. I watched in wonder as she puttered efficiently about the kitchen. "What are you doing?"

"I'm frying your egg. This is a stove. Do you know what a stove is?"

"Should I?"

She explained about stoves and how you mustn't touch the burners because you could get burned.

I pointed to the refrigerator. "What's that?"

"It's a refrigerator. You keep food in it."

"Why?"

"So the food won't spoil."

"Why would it spoil?"

"Because it's warm in the house."

"What is spoil?"

When Harold came home later in the day, I heard the nurse telling him about the endless questions I had been asking. "Better you than me," he said. "I'm all questioned out. I don't know how many more questions I can take."

"Why don't you like me to ask questions?" I asked.

"But he was moving toward the door. " 'Bye now, gotta run . . ."

I had noticed a pile of books that were kept on a separate shelf in the living room. "Why are these books here?"

"That's what you used to use, what you used to teach."

"I was a teacher?"

"I told you at the hospital. Don't you remember? Everybody has told you you were a teacher."

"I know."

"You taught medical assisting and geriatric assisting."

This was getting boring. I changed the subject. But later I proudly showed the nurse the books. "These are *my* books." I wished I could remember that big word to tell her what I taught.

"I know, dear," she said, starting to pick one up.

I snatched it away. "It's mine, damn, damn, damn."

"That's all right, dear. I was only going to look at it."

"Nobody's supposed to look at it." I felt very protective of my special books. "You can look at the other books."

"No thanks, dear. I was just looking."

"I'm not dear. Why do you call me dear? I'm Beverly." I decided I didn't like her anymore. Wasn't she supposed to go home at the end of the week? I wished she would leave now.

As she busied herself around the kitchen, I would grab my books and pretend to read. So many big words, and pictures too, with the parts of the body—inside and out. Did we really look like that? How funny.

I talked to Harold about the pictures. He explained it so nicely, comparing the body to the body of the car that had taken me home from the hospital. The car had all the lines that carried the fuel to the wheels to keep the car running. People had a little fuel tank right there—the tummy—to keep the arms and legs moving. And instead of a fuel line, people had blood vessels and the blood ran around and fed every little thing in the body.

"What if it forgets to feed something?"

"Then that part shuts down and it won't work anymore. That's why you have to eat more than you do. So your fuel line takes care of everybody and doesn't run short—something for Missy Nose and something for Madame Heart, and something for the ten Toe Sisters."

I was laughing. What fun Harold could be! Right then I was glad he was my husband. But other times . . . Why did he have to get grumpy? I decided to test him.

"I don't need a nurse."

"Dr. O'Connor says you need one until you can take care of yourself and the house. She is an LPN. That means Licensed Practical Nurse. That means she isn't qualified to do all the things for you that the nurses in the hospital could do, but she is qualified to take care of you and teach you how to do everything you need to know."

"Why can't *you* teach me?"

"I'm not a babysitter. I'm not a teacher. I'm not an expert on medicine. I barely know what to do with you when you have a tantrum."

I was about to have one now. "I hate you. You don't like me."

He caught my hands. "I don't like you? Why?"

"Because I'm a dummy. Because I can't take care of myself."

"There, there," he pulled me closer. "You don't have to be a dummy forever. Be a smart girl and behave."

Now I was really furious. "See? You think I'm a dummy. You said so. You said so."

"Now, now, I take it back. You're not a dummy."

"Then why won't you teach me?"

"Because I have to go to work." He almost ran to the door. As he opened it, he shouted, "Oh, nurse, will you see what Beverly needs?" And then he was gone.

The nurse appeared, and I made no attempt to hide my hostility. She looked at me as if I were a wild animal. "There, there, Beverly," she said, soothingly. "Everything's going to be all right."

"Harold doesn't like me," I sobbed.

"Yes, he does," she said, patting my shoulder cautiously.

"How do you know?"

"He told me."

"Oh." For a moment I was pleased. But then I was angry again. "You're a liar, a damn, damn liar," I snarled, moving toward her. She backed away.

"Beverly, how would you like to play a game?"

Suddenly I felt as if nothing unpleasant had happened. "Fine. Shall I run and get the cards?"

"Yes, do."

Later I eavesdropped on the nurse and Harold. She was telling him how violently I had behaved, and he promised to try to get me to stop. Harold said sadly, "I'm afraid Dr. O'Connor was right. She wasn't ready to come home yet."

I was terrified. Were they going to send me back? How could I show I was ready to be home? I decided I would be a good girl and not say damn anymore and I would be nice and not scream or cry. Maybe that would show them I was ready to stay home. But something in me longed to be in my nice quiet hospital room, looking out the window at the snowflakes, waiting for Dr. O'Connor to come bounding in with his hearty, "How's my girl? How's Beverly Slater today?"

Why couldn't I be in both places?

"She said that her first memory was of walking around the hospital in the corridors but that the whole of her experience in the hospital was somewhat vague. She remembers that at times she went to what she afterwards realized was an elevator and went downstairs into the lobby of the hospital, attempting to leave. She remembers saying, 'I'm going out,' but remembers not really knowing where she was going—just that she wanted to get away. She told me that she learned later that, after a couple of such attempts, a sign was put on the back of her hospital gown which stated, 'Please return to Neurological ICU.' "

4

Where's Beverly?

"*W*here's Beverly?"

I was hiding. "Shhh," I whispered to my panda. We were behind the sofa. I had tried hiding in the closet but it was too dark in there, too scary. It was different from the darkness outside at night. As long as there were stars, I liked the night's darkness. The stars were my friends. I whispered secrets to them. Like the secret that panda and I were going to run away.

The nurse found me. "Oh, there you are." I could tell she was pretending not to be angry. "Lunch is ready."

"Lunch is ready. Lunch is ready," I mimicked her. "I don't want lunch and I don't have to eat if I don't want to." I knew she wanted to teach me some more of those silly table manners.

Why? When I was in the hospital nobody had said I couldn't pick up my food with my fingers. Here it was a firm rule.

"Mr. Slater says if you don't eat properly he can't take you to the restaurant. Eat." She knew I had been begging to go to a restaurant ever since Harold had first mentioned it.

"Okay, I'll eat if I don't have to use a fork." I had to get some kind of victory out of this situation.

"But if you don't use a fork, he says you can't go to the restaurant. Mr. Slater says no one eats with their fingers in the restaurant."

"Mr. Slater. Mr. Slater. Mr. Slater." I mimicked. "I don't have to do what he says. I don't have to do what you say."

"How would you like to play a game?"

"Goody, shall I get the cards?"

"Just as soon as you use your manners and eat the food on your plate we'll play Fish. Would you like that?" It was a game my granddaughter had taught me—simple and so exciting!

"Okay." Napkin in lap. Pick up fork. Don't put elbow on table. Close mouth to chew. Chew, swallow, chew, swallow. The food had no flavor. I wondered why people thought so highly of it. But it didn't really matter—soon the ordeal was over and the card game had begun.

"Will you tell Harold I used my manners?"

"Of course. You have been very good."

My attention span was not one of my strong points.

"What are we going to do next?"

"I thought we would bake a cake for Mr. Slater's dinner—would you like that?"

"His name is Harold. Call him Harold."

"He is my employer, Beverly. I can't call him Harold until he tells me to."

Funny world.

One of my greatest adventures took place almost immediately after I came home. I was looking at my next-door neighbor's backyard and I saw beautiful yellow things coming out of the grass. I walked over and began pulling at them.

An old man came running out of the house. "Stop, stop," he shouted. "Beverly, what are you trying to do?"

"They're pretty," I said. "What are they?"

"They're flowers, Beverly. They grow in the ground," he continued, seeing my confusion, "and they are to enjoy, not to pick. If you do pick them, you don't just pull off the heads."

"Flowers," I thought. Aha—he was wrong. "There were flowers in the hospital. These aren't red."

"These are yellow. But they are still flowers. There are all kinds of flowers—blue and orange and yellow."

He showed me how to replant them, and he added a little water, "To make it grow. Everything needs water to grow."

"Do *you* need water to grow?"

He chuckled. "Of course, but I'm not doing much growing these days."

"Why?"

"People just grow till they are sixteen or eighteen. Then they just need water to stay healthy."

Now I understood—that was what was wrong with the little people who were my grandchildren. They were going to grow until they were sixteen or eighteen. Why hadn't Harold or someone told me about that? At first I was annoyed, then proud that I had figured it out myself.

But I found a flaw in his story. "Perri doesn't drink water," I said. "Perri drinks milk. You lied to me."

"No, Beverly, I wouldn't lie to you. But let me explain. Milk has a lot of water in it, even if it's white. Your baby granddaughter gets water that has a lot of food in it and it is called milk."

This was getting boring. "I hate milk." I didn't know if I hated it or not but I certainly didn't want to talk about it anymore. I wanted to talk about yellow. I loved yellow. And I especially loved these yellow flowers.

Suddenly my attention was caught by a bird sitting on a limb of a bush. I ran to catch it but it flew away. I started to cry. Why did everything have to be so difficult? "Why can't I play with it? Why didn't it wait for me?"

"Because it's wild. Birds like to be fed, but they don't play with people. Come back tomorrow and we will feed the birds, Beverly. Maybe one will eat from your hand."

"Beverly." It was Harold, calling from the house. "Come to lunch."

I moved toward him but then I ran back to my new friend. "Where do I go?"

He looked a little startled. "Why, knock on my door."

I put out my hand. "My name is Beverly Slater. What is your name?"

"I know you're Beverly. You used to call me Pops. All the neighborhood calls me Pops just like you always did."

"Okay," I said, and I ran home.

Each day was beautiful and bright, a wonderful beginning. Even the rain—which Harold always complained about—seemed a wonderful thing . . . I loved the way it made the ground so shiny, the way the drops felt . . . I ran outside without an umbrella, my face turned up to the sky.

The nurse ran after me, yelling, "You'll catch cold, Beverly. Come take this umbrella."

"Go to hell." I was cussing much less but enjoying it more—I loved seeing how upset it made people. Of course, they always tattled to Harold, who would lecture me and warn me that I'd have to go right back to the hospital if I wasn't a good girl.

I was amazed at the way Midnight moved. Jump, jump and another jump and he had reached the top of the refrigerator, where he sat safely out of my reach.

"You have to be gentle with a cat," the nurse said. "You hold it too tight. You have to be gentle."

I didn't know why I had to be gentle. The cat wasn't gentle. It scratched. It ran away. It ignored me and worst of all, it preferred my grandchildren to me. It was my cat but it preferred the little people. I had to do something. Gradually, I learned to handle the cat the way the nurse said and suddenly it liked me again.

Liked me too much, in fact. It brought me a dead bird. "That's a present," the nurse said. "The bird is a present the cat has brought you. It can't buy you a present, so it finds you one. Isn't that nice?"

"But why isn't the bird moving?"

"Because it is dead. The cat killed it because it wanted to bring you a present."

Horrified, I started crying. Something was all wrong here. I loved birds. Pops had told me all about birds and flowers, but he hadn't said anything about cats catching birds and killing them. He said you couldn't catch a bird.

I ran next door and asked him again, and he explained that people were slow but cats were fast and if they tried very hard, cats could outwit birds and catch them by pouncing on them.

When I got back home, the dead bird was gone and Midnight was out of sight. The next time he got generous, he brought me a mouse.

I had no particular feeling about the fact that this was a mouse. I just wanted to touch it. But Harold snatched it away from me and flipped it into the wastebasket.

"But it's a present to me," I said. "It's mine."

"Oh, God," he groaned, holding his head in his hands. "Oh,

God, how long?" Then he explained that mice were dirty, often disease carriers, and they stole food people wanted to eat.

"But there was a nice mouse in a story I read."

"Well, this is real life." A moment later he was telling the nurse, "Can you imagine a woman who *likes* mice? In the old days she'd have been screeching and yelling, 'Harold, get it away from me.' I sometimes think I'm living in a nightmare and I'm going to wake up."

"I know, I know how you must feel," she said. "I get a little bit of it and I know how you must feel."

I hated her and the sympathy in her voice. It was okay for Harold to talk about me—but not to *her*.

Those first nights I was back from the hospital I asked Harold to come outside with me every time the sky was clear. When I tilted my head back and looked at the stars, I almost felt that I could fall into the heavens. Harold wasn't particularly pleased. "That's not healthy thinking, babe. You've got enough problems without creating new ones."

I tried again. "What keeps them from falling down?"

"Some do. I'll get you a book."

I had the same question about airplanes.

"Some do. I'll get you a book."

I was getting quite a collection of books.

Harold spent hours answering my questions, often repeating the answer several times a day. It was all pretty hit-and-miss—sometimes I couldn't seem to hang on to the simplest answer, and other times I could understand and retain a sophisticated concept.

I kept taking down my teaching books and looking at them. I couldn't believe I had once known everything in them.

"What did I teach?"

"Ah, good," Harold said. "I've been waiting for you to ask. We all tried to explain at the hospital, but you weren't interested. You were teaching geriatrics when you had the accident."

"What's geriatrics?"

"That has to do with growing old."

"Was I teaching people how to grow old?"

"No, you were teaching medical assistants and secretaries how to handle the elderly patients. All the special medical problems older people have when they get sick."

"Oh."

"And I think you were teaching some other courses as well."

But I was no longer interested in the subject. I was leading Harold to a door. My closet door. "Who do these belong to?" I asked for the umpteenth time.

"They are yours, dear. You can put on anything you want. But Joanie is going to show you what colors you can wear together."

"Does she have to give permission?"

"Of course not. I mean she'll show you what looks pretty together."

Maybe that's why I hated what the nurse was picking for me to wear. Joan would make it pretty. Joan had given me an old red blouse that she was wearing. I had wanted it—demanded is more like it—and she had taken it off.

Every visitor taught me a little bit more about the old Beverly. Soon after I'd left the hospital, a woman I didn't recognize rang the bell. "Hello, who are you?" I asked, always happy to have a visitor.

"Beverly, we used to share rides to school, take turns driving. We taught in the same school."

"I *know* I was a teacher," I said, irritably. How dumb did she think I was?

She went on and on about the schools I had taught in. Names, names. It was boring. I was glad when she left. Afterward, I couldn't even remember her name and Harold had to remind me—Evelyn Portnoy.

I was much happier when the children visited. Once, as Perri and I played on the floor, my father talked about what I had been like as a little girl . . . How I would run to meet him every night after work at the streetcar stop . . . How he always had something for me hidden in one of his pockets, and of course I always found it . . .

Perri and I were fascinated by the idea of these magical pockets. What was hidden in them? "Sometimes bubble gum. Lollipops. Sometimes a yo-yo or a set of jacks. Sometimes a jump rope or hair ribbons."

"What else? What else?"

"Sometimes Cracker Jack, sometimes licorice sticks. Sometimes a little celluloid doll before they even had Barbie dolls."

"What else did you bring? What else?"

"Once I brought real lipstick by mistake and your mother couldn't get it off. You painted yourself like an Indian on the warpath. On your nose. On your forehead. She was plenty mad at me."

We laughed and laughed. This one they didn't have to explain. I was already wearing lipstick. Joanie, Erma, and Shirley had all shown me how to put it on.

I still marveled at everything. Furniture that was shiny. Soft things that were fluffy. I played a follow-the-leader touching game with my granddaughter—"Touch the window. Touch the chair. Touch the top of the stairs." Whoever was It ran here and there touching things, and the person following—usually me—had to touch whatever the leader touched.

I especially loved the circular stair in the foyer. You could go up five steps and be in the living room or down five steps and be in the family room. "Touch the top step. Touch the bottom step. Touch the second step." It was fun. I was proud of how quickly I obeyed the commands. There was only one I wouldn't follow. "Touch the closet." Aryn would run in, but I wouldn't. I was still afraid.

After a while, it seemed as if no one liked me. The nurse didn't like me, Harold didn't like me . . . But at least Midnight liked me. And I liked him. Then he brought me a third present. Another mouse. Since mice were so nasty, I had decided I didn't like them after all. The presents had to stop. I was crying.

"Please, cat," I said, "no more presents." The presents stopped. Midnight seemed to understand me better than Harold, and surely better than that hateful old nurse.

Gradually I realized that there was someone else who didn't like me. Stuart.

I could feel it. Whenever he came to visit he would sit around, just looking at me, not saying much. Not smiling, not encouraging me.

I had not yet relearned subtlety. "You don't like me," I said. "If you don't like me, I don't like you."

"Oh, mother, I like you, I like you."

"No, you don't. What's the matter with me?" I was always seeking approval, always wanting to be liked.

"Nothing's the matter with you. I just can't get over the changes and the way you talked to me in the hospital. But don't worry about it."

"How did I talk to you in the hospital?"

"Don't you remember your cussing me out all the time? Don't you remember your foul language? Even the guys I run around with don't use such filthy language. It does something when you hear your own mother talking like that."

"There were tears in his eyes and I felt awful. I didn't know what to do. Should I take his hand? They said he was my child and yet I felt that *he* was the older and wiser one. He was a stranger, a stranger who disapproved of me.

"If I promise not to say it again, will you quit being mad at me?"

"I'm not *mad* at you, mother." Yes, he certainly had that older and wiser look. "Okay, if you promise to quit swearing, I'll promise to not be mad at you."

Solemnly, we shook hands. I looked at this person in awe, this handsome man with the mustache and dark hair. Was this my child?

A woman named Roz called and asked when would I be well enough to play tennis again with my old gang.

"What's tennis?"

That seemed to throw her. "It's a game."

"I don't know anything about that game."

"It's easier if I show you. I'm sure it's like riding a bicycle. Once you know how, you can always do it."

"Oh, do I ride a bicycle?"

"*That* I don't know. You'll have to ask Harold. But you're one heck of a good tennis player. We played doubles a lot."

"Is that a card game?"

"No, I'm still talking about tennis—that's when four people play instead of two. We had a foursome that played at the club."

"Oh. Give me your telephone number and I'll talk to Harold about it."

I was learning to take everyone's phone number. It was fun.

Harold was pleased when I told him about Roz's invitation. He wanted me to be friendlier to old acquaintances. Apparently I had been an avid tennis player and had been taught to play by one of my high school friends. Then I had taken lessons with a pro.

A meeting with me and the "gang" was arranged. Harold took a special interest in this event, carefully selecting my outfit—white shorts, a white knit shirt, and white shoes.

"This doesn't look right," I said.

"Why not?"

"It's not fancy enough. I should wear a pants suit."

"No. Roz talked to me and said this is what all the other girls will be wearing."

"Okay." I shrugged. "It's a funny party." I insisted on wearing a colorful scarf—something to pep up this drab (by my standards, anyway) outfit. Hal tossed a tennis racket and box of balls into the backseat of the car, and as he dropped me off at Roz's, he told me to take them with me.

"Oh," I said, "I thought they were for you. Why do I need them?"

"Don't ask questions. You'll understand everything later." I decided not to argue this one. Anyway, I was sort of looking forward to meeting my "gang."

After lunch, everyone grabbed a racket and off we went to the tennis court. Suddenly I was standing on the court, racket and ball in hand, without the slightest idea why everyone was looking at me expectantly.

"Okay, you've got your racket and your ball," Roz said with authority.

"Okay, I've got my racket and my ball . . . " I looked wildly around the court. "Now what the fuck do I do with them?"

Someone said, "Oh, my," and Roz shushed her.

She showed me. Once. Twice. I tried. I couldn't get the ball over the net. She and the others hit balls to me and I still couldn't get them over the net. Half the time, I couldn't even connect.

Roz looked at me sympathetically.

"I'm sorry. Somehow Harold thought maybe getting involved in the game you loved would bring back your memory."

"I loved this game?"

"You sure did. You took lessons and we reserved a court every week. Usually we played doubles with your friends here."

I felt like the dummy again and I hated it. I decided I would master this game if it killed me . . . "Well, don't worry," I said, "I'll be playing tennis again. I can do everything I want to. I'm reading and writing now. I can read anything."

I was thinking of the hard medical words I'd learned, but I could tell they saw it as the bragging of a child, because there was something condescending about the way they were looking at me. I wanted to tell them about how I had also learned to put the square peg in the square hole but somehow I realized they wouldn't be particularly interested or impressed.

Roz did take me to the court again, and I managed to hit a few balls but they landed all over the place. I seemed to have no control over this game. At one point, totally frustrated, I tried to hit the ball with my hand.

Harold asked me how I liked tennis. I said I didn't think much of the game but I liked the balls.

He looked puzzled.

"The balls?"

"Oh, yes. They're so pretty—green, yellow, orange."

So much for tennis.

5

Out of the House and into the World

I kept hearing about restaurants, but Harold said it was too soon to go to one. Instead he would take me to see his sister. "You have a sister?"

"Don't you remember my sister and her husband came to see you the very first day you were home from the hospital?"

"I guess so." I really didn't. "And they came to the hospital."

"No, Beverly, they did not come to the hospital. I told them not to come. You wouldn't have known them and they wouldn't have appreciated the language you were using." Vaguely I understood that I was supposed to be insulted—he had been protecting them from me—but I didn't care. The important thing was that he was taking me visiting. An adventure.

"I told you about her. Elaine. She's your sister-in-law."

"Oh, goody. Let's go. Let's go." I was excited—not because I was going to meet a relative, but because it meant a car ride, a new adventure. Anything new thrilled me. And I especially loved going to new houses.

Elaine's was a detached house, brick on the first floor and siding on the second floor. I didn't really like it. As soon as we got inside, I told her so. "I like my house better than your house."

She and Harold looked at each other. Harold shrugged. "She's going to charm school to learn tact." Elaine smiled, and the tension was broken.

At first I didn't really recognize Elaine or her husband. I looked closer. Elaine had such curly hair—just like Harold's—blondish, with just a little gray in it. And Marvin was taller and heavier than Harold. (Harold had become the yardstick against whom I measured all males.)

The living room was done in soft beiges and browns, all very subdued. So were Elaine's clothes. It certainly was a sharp contrast to my red outfit. "Why don't you wear red?" I asked her. "I like red or yellow."

Before Elaine could answer, Harold broke in. "Well, you're looking at the kind of colors you used to wear, and I like them. They're called conservative." I could tell he was annoyed, but I decided to ignore him.

I went exploring with Elaine, who explained what things were and why this or that was on the wall and why the chair was here rather than over there. I had opinions about everything and of course offered them freely. I approved of her fireplace, I told her, because I had a fireplace in my family room.

But suddenly I stopped dead in my tracks. On the floor in front of me was a beautiful carved black lacquered plant stand. I sat down and examined it.

"Can I have it?" I said in my sweetest voice. "It's so pretty."

I heard Harold's warning voice.

"Beverly. You don't ask for things in people's homes."

Elaine was gently explaining that the table had been willed to them by Marvin's mother. I didn't know what difference that made. "That means it's yours and you can give it to anyone you want. Isn't that what it means?"

But Elaine was apologetic. "You see, dear, it has sentimental value because his mother loved the little table and wanted him to have it."

Harold was pulling me toward the door, away from my beloved table.

"We have to be leaving, Elaine. I think I haven't allowed enough time yet before going visiting with this little girl."

I wanted to stay. Elaine assured me that I could come see the table again soon.

I was furious. Now Harold refused to stop at a restaurant. "I told you, you're not ready."

"What is ready? You said table manners!"

"Ready is when you don't make a scene like you just did. I don't know what you would do in a restaurant. Ready is when you obey me better. If I signal you that this is a no-no, you must stop doing it, whatever it is. You knew I didn't want you to keep pestering my sister for her table. That wasn't nice."

The next time Harold ventured to take me to his sister's I still could not keep away from the plant stand, but this time I thought I handled it very well—I offered to buy it. Unbeknown to Harold, I had brought along a handful of change to cinch the deal!

When that didn't work, I offered to trade her something of mine for it. And again, we were on our way home sooner than planned.

As it turned out, it was not Harold but Shirley and Erma—with Harold's permission, of course—who took me to my first restaurant. He was skeptical about my newest adventure. "Are you sure you can handle it? I won't take responsibility."

"Don't worry," they told him. "It's going to be fine."

In the car, Shirley explained what a restaurant was for, that there would be a lot of people and that I shouldn't be afraid. She said we were going to a lovely seafood place called the Rusty Scupper.

"What's a scupper?"

"I don't know, but it sounds very nautical. We can ask when we get there, if you really want to know."

You bet I wanted to know. The instant we arrived I asked the hostess and she explained that it was a place in the side of a ship to open and let water run out. "Why? Is it rusty? Does it have a lot of nails?" I'd just recently learned the word *rusty* when Harold had shown me a rusty nail in the backyard, and I was thrilled to show it off.

The hostess looked a little apprehensive. "I really couldn't say."

How nice it was to see all those people sitting around! I said hello to everyone who looked my way as we passed. As soon as we sat down, Shirley explained that I didn't have to say hello unless I knew the person. She didn't sound pleased.

She didn't sound pleased. I was crushed. "But Harold said I have to be friendly even if I don't remember her, because she knows me even if I don't know her. He says that's not nice, not to talk."

For a moment they looked confused. "Oh," said Erma. "When you meet people who talk to you, you have to talk to them and be friendly even if you don't know who they are."

"That's right," I said, "because they can help me remember."

Shirley added, "Do you understand now, Bev? You don't talk to them here because you don't know them and they don't know you."

"That's all right," I said. "We'll get acquainted."

Now they were studying the menu. They asked me what I would like.

"I don't care," I said. I couldn't make much sense of all the dishes.

"Would you like sole?" they asked. "Would you like lobster?"

I said "Sure" to everything.

They decided it would be easier to order for me. I ate very carefully, watching my manners as the nurse had taught me to do. Napkin in the lap. Pick up fork. Put down fork before picking up roll. Do not have fork in one hand and roll in other. Butter little piece of roll.

I liked butter. It was smooth, like ice cream, only not so cold. I ate very little, paying more attention to the other tables than to my own. At one point Shirley and Erma had to stop me from going over to talk to someone at a nearby table.

"No, Beverly," Erma said, "you can't leave the table in a restaurant."

"You can if you say excuse me. Excuse me."

"No, you can't go." Shirley was holding my arm. "That's a table of strangers. You don't know them, do you?"

"No, but I think they want to talk to me."

"No, they're just looking around the room, the way you are. I think they're looking for service. See, they wanted wine and now their wine has arrived."

"Oh . . ." How disappointing! Life was *so* complicated. Nothing was as it seemed.

But it wasn't such a bad day. On the way home, Erma bought me a pair of sunglasses. She let me pick the color, and I chose the brightest pair I could find—cerise. It was quite the nicest present I had ever had. Next to the panda.

■ ■ ■

What a wondrous world! I couldn't get over its endless challenges and discoveries . . . Harold took me on a drive to Atlantic City. "You are going to see the ocean."

I stood in the sand, transfixed by the sight of the grand blue sea. It seemed limitless. It stretched to the sky. It stretched as far as the eye could see. It wiggled and wriggled and would not stand still. It made funny noises—*swoosh, swoosh*.

Harold watched me. "What's the matter? Why do you look worried?"

"What makes it stop?"

He paused for a long moment. "I'll be damned. What makes it stop? I never thought of that. The sand. The sand makes it stop."

"Oh, good," I said. "It can't get to me." I ran and touched it. It was surprisingly cool. I rose and ran back to Harold. He was still standing there, shaking his head.

"I swear," he said, "you ask stranger questions than the kids ever did. I raised two kids and now I'm raising a third."

I laughed, happily. I had fallen in love with the seashore. I wanted to stay here forever. Soon I had my shoes off and was running through the sand to the water. How thrilling the sand felt. How thrilling the cold water felt on my toes. But the April sun was hot. Suddenly something grabbed my hand. It was Harold, running along beside me. "Oh what the hell," he laughed, "if you can't change 'em, join 'em."

After some time, we left the beach for our seaside condominium—which, he explained, we rented all year round so that we could enjoy the water in winter, too, even if we couldn't swim in it.

I looked out the window at the water.

"Why not?"

"It gets cold and it gets covered with ice. You remember snow. Remember when you saw it from your hospital window?"

"Oh, yes, it was beautiful. Is that where ice comes from?"

"Oh, God," he groaned, "now what have I started? No, ice is ice and snow is snow."

"I'm no dummy. I know all about ice. You put water in the refrigerator and you take out ice cubes."

"Well that's sort of what the Lord does. He puts down water and if the place is cold enough, you get ocean-size ice cubes."

"Do the fish like it?"

"Wow, do the fish like it. Well, it depends on the fish. Sometimes you get a fish in your ice cube and sometimes you don't. Generally, the fish live under the ice—see, the ice isn't all the way down and it's warmer under the ice. But to answer your question, if the fish don't like it, they go someplace else."

"I know. Like the birds go south. I'll bet you didn't think I knew."

"Who told you? Mr. Ciampi next door?"

"Oh, is that his real name? Oh. He said to call him Pops. Why did he do that?"

"Because that's his nickname and he's known you for a long time—ever since we moved into the neighborhood."

"What difference does that make?"

"Well, you call people you've known for a long time by their first names, and nicknames are like first names."

"What is my mother's first name?"

"Ann." My, how smart he was to know all these things.

"Should I call her Ann?"

"No, because she is your mother. You call special relatives by their titles. You call her mother."

"Shirley is my cousin. Should I call her cousin?"

"Oh, give me strength. No, Beverly, continue to call her Shirley. A cousin is not a close relative like a mother."

"Isn't a husband a close relative?"

"No, Beverly, you may continue to call me Hal. I'm only a close relative through marriage, and that doesn't count."

"Oh, I'm so confused."

"You're confused? Well, you're getting me confused. I'm going for a short walk to clear my mind. Be a good girl and stay right here and I'll be back. Sit." Obediently, I sat down on the yellow rug.

But right after he left, I ran to the door to follow him. It was locked. I knew about keys. I tried to find one. No luck. I plopped down on a sofa and sulked.

When he came back he had a book for me, a children's book, all about the world around us and why this was so and that was so. I pored over that book for hours, happy to see I wasn't the only one who needed answers.

When we got home, I announced that I was going to write a letter. "Fine," said Harold, a little surprised. "Who do you want to write it to?"

I looked at the pile of bills and get-well cards on the kitchen table and said, "I don't know. You tell me."

"Who has been good to you?"

"You have. I'll write you a letter."

"No. You don't have to write me a letter. I live here. You write the letter to someone who doesn't live here but who comes to see you and does nice things for you."

"Who is that?"

"I don't know. You tell me. It's *your* letter."

Suddenly I thought of Erma. She was always so nice to me, coming over every day and taking me for rides and to look at stores. And she had bought me those pretty sunglasses.

"Can I write a letter to Erma?"

"Sure, that's a fine choice. She and her family love you very much."

"Will you help me write the letter?"

"Let the nurse help you. I've got to get back to work."

"No, I want *you* to help me." I was starting to cry.

"Okay, stop blubbering. I'll help you."

"Can I use my pretty cards?"

"Of course. That's what they're there for." Someone had brought me a little box of folded notepaper with huge butterflies on each in my favorite color—yellow.

I used card after card until finally I got it right. Harold helped me. Though he didn't know that Erma spelled her name with an *E*, I thought it summed up very nicely how we felt about friendship . . .

> Dear Irma and Family:
>
> My love to all of you for helping me get from 1 day to the next day.
>
> Irma, you are very close to my heart and I can never leave you
>
> You are my family and I love you very much. My thanks to you are in my love to you. I need you for the rest of my life.
>
> Love
Bev

I was very proud of my letter and showed it to everyone before handing it to Erma in person when she arrived the next day. I was glad the nurse didn't tattle on me when I took full credit for the letter. Erma promised to keep it forever.

I felt a little guilty. I had written a lot about love in the letter and I still wasn't exactly sure of what it was. But Harold said love was friendship and friendship was love, and Erma didn't seem to find anything wrong with the note, so I decided not to worry.

It was Joan who took me to a large department store for the first time. I was overwhelmed by all the clothes—so much to look at. And so many people to watch and talk to. I didn't know where to look first. Now I was Joanie's child as she led me around by the hand, showing me dress-up clothes and sports clothes and where to look for the size.

I didn't know my size. I thought the saleslady was brilliant to figure out that I was a size eight. I wandered around looking at everything that said eight. I tried on a lightweight coat, liked what I saw, and headed for the exit.

"Aren't you going to take that coat off?" Joanie asked.

"No. I picked it out. It's mine."

"You were trying things on for size. If you want the coat, you have to pay for it."

"But this isn't a grocery store."

"No, it's worse." She laughed. "You have to pay a lot of cabbage for a coat like that." She explained what *cabbage* was.

"Everything's got a nickname. Even money."

"Well, I've got to get home to the kids. Do you want the coat or don't you?"

"I want it. It's mine."

"Not yet. Do you have a charge here? No, I don't recall that you do. If you really want the coat, we'll have to put it on layaway." That was very nice. You didn't have to give them any money—well, just a little money—and the coat was yours and nobody could have it until you came back and brought them more money.

Suddenly clothes were very important to me.

One day I tried on an old outfit at home for Harold. "I don't like it," I said.

"What's wrong with it?"

"The color. It doesn't have any color."

"Sure it has color—it's sort of a light brown. I think you'd call it beige or tan."

"I don't like it. I don't like anything here."

"These are expensive. They cost a lot of money. And you have to wear something."

"No, I don't. I'll wear this red blouse Joanie gave me."

"You bought everything in here—*picked* it all yourself."

"No, I didn't. That was some other lady. I don't know her and I don't like what she picks. You can phone her to come get her clothes."

I knew that was a low blow. He winced. "Would that I could."

I started to cry. It hurt to know that he preferred the other Beverly. He hugged me. "There, there. "We'll go shopping and get you something red or yellow or whatever you want. Okay?"

"Okay. Can we go now?"

"I have an appointment on a siding job. Well, I'll just call the man and make it for tomorrow. You come first."

I couldn't have cared less about Harold's job appointments. So what if the man got angry and said, "You promised to be here today"? I overheard Harold trying to explain that he had a sick wife. After a few minutes of silence I heard him say, "I'm sorry you feel that way about it."

"That's the second job I lost out on this week," he said as he hung up. "Well, come on. Maybe this will jog your memory." He seemed a little sad as he led me to the car. "When I get you squared away, I'm going to have to really get on the ball and earn some money," he said. "I'm eating up our little savings."

"What's savings?" I asked.

"That's money you put away for a rainy day. Your accident was our rainy day." He was silent for a moment. "But I didn't expect a tornado, a hurricane, a flood."

"You're mad at me because I made it rain."

"No, no. Babe, I love you very much. I guess you don't know how I feel about you. Maybe you'll never know. But I'm going to make you happy and maybe I'll even help you remember how the other Beverly loved me and felt about me."

"I don't want to hear about the other Beverly. To hell with Beverly." A passing couple stared at me.

"Okay, don't cry. We'll just talk about the colors you want to wear." We got into the car.

I prattled on and on about the colors and, for the moment, forgot about the other Beverly. I liked everything bright, it seemed, and Harold had to enlist the aid of the clerk to help me understand that ladies generally picked the outfit they liked best—not *everything* they took to the little booth to try on.

I had come for a red skirt and jacket but I left in a bright blue pants suit. The old dignified Beverly had usually worn skirts. The new Beverly liked only pants suits. From then on, only at Harold's insistence would I put on a skirt—usually to visit his family or friends. I didn't care if Shirley or Erma wore skirts—I liked wearing pants.

On the way out of the department store, we passed a makeup counter where a beautiful blond beautician was demonstrating a new line of cosmetics. Soon I had all but disrupted the proceedings, demanding to know what she was doing and what that stuff was in her hand. Harold tried to quiet me down but I ran up and down the aisle picking up this item and that, opening lipsticks, playing with eye pencils.

Customers and clerks were looking at me as if I were crazy—after all, only a crazy person wouldn't know what mascara was.

"I'm not a dummy," I protested, in answer to their looks. "I just never saw this before."

Harold jumped in. "My wife is the victim of amnesia. She's just come out of the hospital and she can't remember all this."

"The other Beverly didn't have this," I protested. "She only had dumb lipstick."

"She's right," he said. "My wife only wore lipstick. I guess there isn't any of this stuff around the house."

Now all the clerks and even some customers, friendly and curious, were clustering around Harold and me, telling Harold what color tones would look good on my face. The beautician had just finished up with someone else. I couldn't believe how beautiful the woman looked. "Can you fix me? Can you fix me?" I demanded, almost jumping up and down. "Can you put all that on me just like her?"

The customers urged Harold to let me be made up. "All right," he sighed, "I hope this doesn't break the bank."

"You only pay for any products she buys," the beautician said.

As she worked she talked aloud to the crowd, "See how this erases the lines under the eyes and those deep indentations?" She was smearing something from my nose to the corners of my lips. I was impressed. I hadn't realized anything needed erasing. "Now this blusher to complement her dark coloring . . ."

When she finished, I looked in the mirror and fell in love with my new face. I wanted every product she had used, including a pair of false eyelashes. Again, Harold sighed deeply and quipped that he only wanted a wife—not someone who looked younger than his daughter.

I was happy. I wanted everyone to see me. When I got home I phoned the children, Shirley, and Erma and told them all to come quick.

The next day I tried to put on my new face myself. It wasn't easy. Again, I used the phone. I was beginning to understand—*this* was what children and friends were for. What could I do for them in return? I hadn't the foggiest. Ever since I'd gotten home from the hospital, everyone had been taking me to lunch to get me out of the house and back into the world. It didn't occur to me that I could take *them* to lunch. That would come later.

Now I had coloring on my face, but I noticed something else amiss. Everyone had such pretty hair. Erma's was dark, almost black. Shirley had pretty yellow hair, like corn on the cob. She called it *blond*.

I began complaining about my hair—it wasn't any particular color and it had these little strands of gray in it, like the ghost lady who had come to see me in the hospital.

"That's because your rinse is all gone," Shirley said.

"Well, of course it's gone," I said. "I rinse my hair and I dry it."

They laughed and explained that I had always used a light reddish rinse that took out the gray and gave my mousy-colored hair just a touch of color.

"Oh, I love red. Could I have it again?"

When I looked at my hair after the rinse, I still wasn't happy. It wasn't red enough. I wanted *really* red hair. I knew what *really* red was because I had seen a woman with bright hair on the street and I had stopped her and asked her what color it was.

She had looked at me a little strangely like she was about to run and I had quickly added, "I would like to have hair just like you, so I wonder what color it is."

Then she'd smiled. "Well, red, obviously—but it's just something my hairdresser puts together. He won't give me the formula."

Aha, so it was all very scientific. I thanked her.

I went right home and told Harold about it. He laughed. "If that's what it takes to make you happy, you shall have a formula."

Soon a male beautician came to the house, cut my hair, and applied color. "Are you sure it is red?" I kept asking him. "I don't want it to be *almost* red. I want it to be *really* red like that picture you showed me. That looks like the girl I saw on the street with the pretty red hair."

"You don't want it to be too red," he said. "You don't want it to be harsh and artificial. You want just a nice red shade that will look good with your skin tones." I was sure he was just humoring me the way Harold did, and that my hair would turn out like the wash or rinse or whatever it was—anyway, all washed out.

But when I saw my hair, I was delighted. Short and curly and *really* red.

Harold looked at me and said, "Oh, my! I guess you really *are* a different person."

"Do you like it?"

"It's different."

"Do you like it?"

"It'll do."

"Harold! Do you like it?"

"I love it. I like it. It's great. And now you're the next Rita Hayworth."

"Who's she?"

"The love goddess in movies we used to go to when we were courting. I think you were jealous of her because I liked her a lot."

"Oh, shut up." It was my new phrase when I was annoyed and couldn't think of what else to say.

" 'Shut up' is almost as bad as cussing, Bev; why don't you say 'Oh, beans.' "

"Oh, beans, beans, beans. I hate string beans."

"That childishness doesn't go well with your nice new hair," he said.

"Oh, beans, go to hell, you bastard."

"Uh-oh, temper, temper. Remember, we don't cuss anymore."

"You cuss. I hear you."

"Well, men are different. They're supposed to cuss, but ladies aren't."

"I'm not a lady. You said I'm a child."

"So I did. But for Christ's sake, start growing up."

"Will you like me better?"

"A lot better."

Sometimes when I was really acting up, Harold would play his trump card. "Beverly, if you can't learn to act like a civilized person and stop this violence and this swearing, you will have to go back to the hospital."

"Why? What would they do?"

"I don't know. That's their problem. Dr. O'Connor said if I couldn't cope with you, I had to bring you back. You heard him."

"Okay. I'm good now. I'm a good girl."

"Oh, now you're a good girl, but are you going to stay a good girl?"

"Sure, Harold. I promise." I was sniffling a little.

He patted me on the back as he hugged me. "There, there."

"You're not going to take me back, are you?"

"No, Beverly, not now that you're a good girl."

As I picked up clues from Shirley and Erma, I was learning to act like an adult. But at home with Harold, whenever I became frustrated, it was as if the other person inside of me—the little child from the hospital days—reemerged. I named her Little Beverly.

Little Beverly took over whenever I didn't like the directions I was being given by Harold. Little Bevie didn't have to do anything she didn't want to do. Little Bevie didn't care if you called her dumb. She just hugged her panda and shut out the world.

She wanted to go back to the hospital and have her own room and have nice Dr. O'Connor come in and boom at her, "Hello, Beverly, how's my girl today?" That had been the good, safe world.

But the other me, the Beverly trying to grow up fast, had a terrible fear of having to go back to the hospital and being kept there. Every time Harold mentioned that it was getting to be time for my checkup, I wanted to run away.

Sometimes, when I was alone in the house, full of fear, I wondered why I had lived through this accident. Wouldn't it have been easier to die? Little Bevie didn't want to meet all these strangers in her life—she had panda. Little Bevie's world had become "adult" Bev's emotional sanctuary.

I was determined to learn everything about the kitchen as fast as I could because Harold had made it clear that the nurses would stay as long as I needed help around the house. I watched the nurse like a hawk and made her let me help her until I got the hang of it.

The first nurse stayed just one week and slept in the guest room. The second week a different nurse came and I continued my histrionics. I learned basic hygiene—bathing and tooth care. Basic cooking included how to look up things in the cookbook. I learned how to solve problems of dressing—how to zip a zipper in the back, how to button blouses, how to put on stockings without the heel ending up on the toe.

I was not exactly the most grateful student. "This is my house and I don't want you," I told the second nurse.

"But you need me, Beverly," she said, looking at me with distaste.

"No, I don't," I said, feeling the same. "I'm big now and I can do everything."

Harold got tired of hearing the nurse's and my complaints and at the end of the second week he agreed to let me try to handle the house alone. Two women under one roof, he said, were impossible to handle. Thus ended the reign of the nurses.

At first, I was ecstatic to be in complete possession of *my* house, with no one hovering over me, telling me what to do. But suddenly I realized I was lonely, not having anyone to fight with. I was not alone for long. Harold would find reasons to come home just to check up on me.

One of the ways I occupied myself was by copying pages of my old teaching books. I didn't understand what it meant but I would copy each page about three times, and gradually some of the ideas would start to make sense. Things about the body. Things about a doctor's office and how you helped him take care of patients and keep his books.

I wasn't sure exactly why I wanted to transcribe the information in the books except that I knew I yearned to understand everything I had understood before. I was determined to show Harold and everyone who came to the house that I was not a dummy.

I tried my hand at cooking. Harold gagged on one of my first efforts. "What's the matter?" I asked, alarmed.

"Salt," he gasped. "Do you realize how salty this is? My God, don't you taste it as you cook?"

"What does *salty* mean?"

"Taste this," he held it toward me. "Do you mean that doesn't taste salty to you?"

"I don't know. I don't know what salty means."

That's when it dawned on him. "You don't taste food, do you? It's time for your checkup, anyway. Wait till Dr. O'Connor hears *this!*"

"I was impressed with the degree of frustration which Mrs. Slater feels. She told me that she cries a great deal, feels alone, and stated, "I feel like I'm alone. I don't really know what a family is. I only know what everybody told me." There appears to be a marked labile quality to Mrs. Slater's emotional tone so that, at times, she can be extremely happy and, as I mentioned earlier, over-enthusiastic and, at other times, particularly when she is by herself, she appears to be depressed and cries a great deal."

6

Strangers

I didn't want to go back to the doctor. Harold said it was only a checkup, but I remembered all too well what Dr. O'Connor had said: if it didn't work out with me at home, Harold could bring me back. I knew I'd been a bad girl and I knew a trick when I saw one.

I was afraid to accuse Harold of what he was doing or even let on that I knew. But I could be clever . . . On the way to Dr. O'Connor's office, I picked a fight over his driving. "I don't want to drive with you. I'm getting out."

"Well, wait until after the bridge. Just behave on the bridge." He was holding me with one hand and driving with the other.

Then I knew—he was afraid I would jump off. Once we were on the bridge, I fought like a tiger to get out. The car veered back and forth as he struggled to stay on the road. At last, as if reading my mind, he yelled. "I won't let them take you back to the hospital." I relaxed and settled down in my seat like a good little girl.

I began chattering about all the things around me. "Oh, isn't that car pretty," and "Oh, look at the lady's dress—I wish I had it. See in the car next to us . . ." When I looked at Harold he was wet with sweat, breathing heavily.

"God, I could have had an accident," he was muttering over and over, "I could have gone over the bridge."

I knew that he had every right to make them take me back to

the hospital. "Don't forget your promise," I said, clutching his arm and cuddling against him as he drove. "I'm going to be very good. You'll see."

"Oh, yeah, oh, I'm sure."

So this was Dr. O'Connor's office. It was on the eleventh floor, and was so elegant, so formal. It frightened me. There were huge overstuffed couches, comfortable chairs, and looming over it all was an enormous ceiling photograph of Independence Hall.

Harold promised to take me to Independence Hall if I behaved myself while Dr. O'Connor examined me. And he promised to give me a book that explained all about the big picture—and the founding fathers. America had not always been the way it was now, he said. The founding fathers rode on horseback. I too, had once ridden on horseback. It was a marvelous new thought.

The two girls behind the desk in the waiting room smiled as I peppered them with personal questions. Obviously someone had prepared them for me. "Do you have a husband?" "Are you happy?" "Why do you wear that thing?"

"This blouse?" one replied, smiling. "Why do you ask?"

"I don't like it," I said. "It's ugly."

Harold pulled me onto one of the large striped sofas that matched the walls. I had never been in a room like this. One wall was brown and one wall was blue and one wall was all mural. I meant to ask Dr. O'Connor what it all meant, but as soon as we were in his office, Harold was telling him about my disastrous cooking.

First the doctor gave me something in a bottle to smell. "How does that smell?" I sniffed it a few times. "I don't know."

"Don't you notice anything? Does it make your eyes burn a little or sting your nose?"

"No, I don't notice anything."

He gave me several other things to sniff with equally dismal results. Then he gave me things to taste. "Does this taste sweet?"

"What does that mean?"

"How does it taste?"

"I don't know. It just melts in my mouth."

"That's sugar and it tastes sweet. Do you like it?"

"Not particularly."

"Now this is salt."

I ate almost a teaspoon. Nothing. It dissolved just like the sugar.

Dr. O'Connor explained to Harold that the sense of smell is closely tied to the sense of taste and that apparently the backlash of my head hitting the pavement had destroyed the olfactory nerves—nerves that fan through the skull in little fibers, moving toward the area at the base of the nose. Once destroyed, the olfactory nerves do not regenerate.

"I'm afraid her sense of taste and smell are permanently gone."

Harold looked a little distressed, then nodded his head thoughtfully. "Well, doctor, at least she can't remember what she's missing. She has no memory of taste or smell. But how can I get her to eat more? She doesn't care for food."

The solution was to find textures I enjoyed, and then to find some nutritious foods of those textures. Vitamins and minerals could be supplemented in pill form.

With Dr. O'Connor, I was all smiles. He seemed very pleased with my progress. For a while he and Harold sat around talking about the brain, how no one could predict what was going to happen to me. I listened with interest and then growing annoyance as the doctor discussed the brain as such a mysterious thing that we never know what might happen after brain injury. Sometimes the senses or the memory flickered off and then back on again. And sometimes it worked the other way—they flickered on and then back off, as in the case of my remembered dressmaker. The light had gone back off. Was it off forever? No one knew.

"Why doesn't he know anything?" I complained to Harold as we left. "I want to go to a doctor who knows."

Harold looked sad.

"Well, you won't find one. He's a top neurosurgeon. This is the last frontier of medicine. Dr. O'Connor said he wrote a paper on memory many years ago and nothing much has changed since he wrote it."

"What do you mean, nothing has changed?"

"Nothing much more is known. It's still a great mystery."

I found vegetables and fruits with textures I liked and I took my vitamins religiously. One time I ran out of vitamins and was instantly sure I was getting weak.

"They don't work that fast," Harold explained. "It takes a while for them to start helping you and it takes a while after you quit taking them for you to start feeling run-down. It's not an instant reaction, Beverly. I'll get the pills in the next few days."

"No, no, I must have them immediately. They work differently on me. Really." I pestered him until he took me to get the new supply and right after I'd taken one I said, "Oh, I feel so much better."

Harold laughed and shrugged. "I'm sure."

Sometimes I felt like a bug on a pin. I was always being studied and analyzed. By the kids, by the doctor, by friends, by Harold. One day Harold said, "I've made a great discovery about you, kiddo. I must call Dr. O'Connor and tell him—maybe it has significance."

"What do you mean?"

"I suddenly realized you have the same biases and fears as before, even though you can't remember them. Take onions. You won't eat raw onions even though you can't taste them. Right? Why won't you eat raw onions?"

"I don't know. I just don't like them."

"Aha . . . see? There's no reason for it. You can't taste them, right? They don't burn your mouth, do they?"

"Of course not. Nothing happens—I just don't like them. I don't know why."

"Aha, aha, and it's the same with heights. You won't go out on any balcony because you can't stand to look down a few stories. And you know what happened at Hoover Dam."

Hal told me that he had long ago taken me on a vacation trip to Las Vegas and Hoover Dam, where he had been thrilled by the sound of the rushing water and the sheer height of the fall—700 feet. He had stopped the car and jumped out to get a glimpse of the view, but I had cowered in the front seat, refusing to move. "Please don't go near it," I had pleaded. "Please get back in. Please let's get away from here."

This fascinated me—I *wasn't* that different from the old Beverly after all . . .

Friends and family never stopped probing. "So now you live in your *own* home. Do you like it?" I knew they wanted me to say how wonderful it was, but as usual I was painfully honest.

"Yes, I guess so. But it's not the hospital."

That would always stun them. "You liked the hospital?"

"I didn't know it then, but I liked it."

"Then why were you trying to get out? You were driving us crazy with your begging to get out."

"Because I was waiting for adventure."

"Adventure?"

"I didn't know what home was. I wanted to go there because everybody talked about it—home. But there was more adventure at the hospital. Nothing happens at home."

I was wrong about that. There was *one* kind of adventure I could be having at home—sex. But I wasn't interested. To me, adventure was seeing new things, exploring new places, seeing strange people. Once I had fully explored my house, I was ready to move on.

I was always begging Harold to take me to new places. We explored Philadelphia—its historic shrines, the restaurants. All of this took time away from Harold's work but I didn't know that, and wouldn't have cared anyway.

During the first few days, I could see now and then that there was something on Harold's mind, but he wouldn't tell me exactly what it was. It had to do with sleeping—that much was clear. "We're going to be very close, he said, and you're going to enjoy it," he kept telling me.

"What am I going to enjoy?"

"The doctor said to take it easy and wait a while before I do it. But don't worry, it won't hurt."

Oh, oh . . . It wasn't going to hurt and a doctor was involved. That meant it *was* going to hurt, and I began to dread it. Sometimes Harold would invite himself to come and stay in my bed until I fell asleep. Sometimes he tried to throw the panda out of the bed, but I wouldn't let him. "No, no, you'll hurt her."

Hal was not happy on these occasions. Often he would say, "Oh, my God, I'm sleeping with a forty-eight-year-old virgin."

"What's a virgin?"

"I'll explain when you're not a virgin anymore."

I looked up the word in an old dictionary . . . "an unmarried woman . . . a maid . . . clean; not soiled, as in *virgin* snow." That wasn't much help.

Harold kept hinting that something momentous lay ahead. It made me nervous. "What are you going to do?"

"We're going to play a game—a game that the doctor wants us to play."

Again, the doctor.

"Why do I have to play the game?"

"Because it's good for you and good for me. It's a game of love."

"Do I have to play?"

"Not if you don't want to, but you'll like this game."

"How does this game go?"

"You try to make the man fit into the woman—this pole into a woman's secret hole."

I laughed. "I know that game—fit the square peg into the round hole." I thought Hal would find this very funny. He didn't. He jumped out of bed muttering, "That does it," and went into the other room. I fell asleep, hugging my panda.

So I was safe from the game of love—at least for a while. But Hal didn't wait too long before trying again. I had many dodges. "I don't like this game." "I'd rather play cards." "I'd rather play with my panda." "I'm reading a book." "I'm studying."

"How can you be studying when you're in bed with your eyes closed?"

"I know. I'm memorizing. I'm thinking."

Eventually I gave in and tried the game. It wasn't exactly thrilling. "You have to move," Hal kept telling me. "You have to move toward me when I move toward you." It was too complicated. Too complicated to be fun. Where was the game?

Afterwards Hal held me in his arms and patted me. "It will be better as we go along. You'll see. You'll awaken sexually and be wanting to play this game all the time."

I doubted it. "How often do you want to play?"

"Very often. Every few days at least. This is why people get married. This very thing—this very game. On our honeymoon, we played this game all night."

I felt sorry for that other Bev. How bored she must have been. I ran down the list of people I knew—"Do they play this game?"

"Everybody."

It was hard to believe. But I figured I had better play the game, too, and sometimes I felt a little stirring but I was still not impressed. This was obviously a man's game, like football— women just watched from the sidelines.

I tried everything to avoid it. I sat reading in a chair until I fell asleep. I sat in the bathtub making bubbles with my bubble bath. Once, I even tried hiding under the bed with my panda.

I tried running out of the house into the night, but after walking up and down the street for a while, I'd get bored and come home. Hal would pretend he didn't notice. And I would be safe for another night.

Sometimes it all seemed like an elaborate hoax. Was there a place for me somewhere, where I would be safe from this game of love? Was Harold the man I really belonged to? Were those really my children?

There was a stranger in my bed, claiming to be my husband. There were strangers in my house, claiming to be my children. There were strangers who came to visit, claiming to be my friends. What was I to do? Was there a place I belonged? A person I belonged to? I looked to the strangers around me for the answers —and found none.

As for Harold, one minute I would try to hold his attention, almost cry for it, and the next I would fly into a rage and try to hit him or run away. I resented his playing the role of husband, father, housemate . . . Somehow I wanted to be free of him, on my own. Of course, I couldn't make a single decision on my own but I resented his power over me and I rebelled in any way I could—very often with my most potent weapon was my lack of interest in sex.

But I tried to show him that in all other respects I was a good wife—a good housekeeper, a good cook. Wasn't that enough? All my friends mentioned how neatly I was keeping the house. But my cooking was still quite another matter. Now Harold found excuses not to come home for dinner.

As for my eating habits, I was doing my best to balance my diet. Some things were smooth, some gritty, and some crunchy. I especially liked the crunchy skin of fried chicken, and cooked it often. But then I read that the skin was fattening and loaded with cholesterol, so I started cutting it off the chicken before cooking it. Even after cooking and cleaning, there were a million other ways for me to avoid sex. I'd do anything—lunching with Erma and Shirley, copying pages of my books, visiting, being visited, lagging behind in restaurants to talk to strangers . . .

Whenever we went out to eat, Hal could hardly keep me at my table. I would see some interesting-looking people and jump up to go over to them. "Hello, I'm Beverly Slater. Who are you? Can I sit with you? I like to meet new people because I don't remember many people. Have you been to the museum? I went to the museum yesterday. Harold took me . . ." But by this time Harold was usually at my side, apologizing for the intrusion.

Only occasionally did they seem glad to see us go. Most couples were curious after they'd heard about my amnesia and would insist that we join them for the rest of the meal. Needless to say, Harold was not exactly enthusiastic about my restaurant behavior.

My usual eating habits often caused quite a stir. Once, in a Chinese restaurant, I found that I was enjoying the texture of a little pot of condiment, so I ate every bit of it. The waitress looked alarmed. "How do you feel?"

"I feel fine. How are you?"

She stared—first at me, then at Harold. "Do you know, you just ate hot mustard?"

"Oh," I said. "Shouldn't I?"

Harold tried another tactic in his campaign to get me interested in sex.

"Do you know why a man and woman come together in bed for sex?"

"No. Why?"

"Because they love each other."

"You'll have to explain about love."

"Love is taking care of someone, the way I take care of you."

"But I don't take care of you. So I don't love you."

"Yes, you do. You cook. That's taking care of me."

"Does that mean the waitress loves you and wants to come together with you in bed?"

Harold laughed. "At least she's in love with my bankroll and she'd like to come together with some of that money." I laughed, too, pretending to understand.

But all this laughter wasn't getting me ready for lovemaking. Harold tried backrubs, caressing the backs of my legs. I wanted more but it didn't make me feel particularly sexy.

"I want to make you happy," he said, one morning.

"That's good."

"I want you to make me happy, too."

"That's nice." Suddenly I realized that I didn't know what he was talking about. "How do I make you happy?"

"By playing the game of love, the game of sex. The game I told you about."

"Can I wait till after lunch to play?"

He looked disgusted. "Why after lunch? You don't like food."

"Because Joanie's kids are coming to play with me."

I often ran around the house naked. Harold, at work on his crossword puzzle, would sit looking at me from under lowered brows. "You're just a tease, Beverly. Go put some clothes on."

"What's a tease?"

"It's a girl who parades around naked like you and gets a man all excited, and then says, 'Not tonight, Napoleon.' "

"Oh, so that's a tease?"

"It's one of the nicer names for it."

"But I do let you do that to me—have sex."

"Yes, but you're still a forty-eight-year-old virgin."

I knew it was supposed to be funny, but I felt insulted. Harold kept telling me that soon I would become interested in sex. I wasn't convinced.

"How will you know it?"

"Well, for one thing, you'll be clinging to me and not to a panda."

Now I was *really* insulted. I clung to both of them—sometimes one, sometimes the other, depending on my mood. After all, the panda couldn't buy me things.

Bernice became my best friend during that summer of 1980, when I was still quite a child. She, too, had a place on the beach, and with both our husbands in town for the summer, she agreed to be my beach playmate.

Romp we did, building sand castles, throwing beach balls, running through the surf. I was amazed as Bernice explained how little creatures lived in the seashells. I thought they were stones—she called them houses.

Many men would talk to Bernice, and I would be bashful, not knowing how to join in the conversation. She explained to them about my condition, but I realized by now that people did not want to hear about my hospital experience or what a wonderful man Dr. O'Connor was.

I kept asking her about how to talk to men. "Come along with me," she said. "I'll let you help me on my new job and you'll see how you talk and joke around with people." She was selling picture framing, and I went with her from store to store.

I soon got the hang of it, making quips and being a little aggressive in pushing shopkeepers to order our wares. I loved it. I loved the excitement—and the money.

One day Bernice said, "I think you're ready to go to a party. I'm inviting some friends and you're to dress up in a party dress and knock on my door at the right time." She helped me pick the dress—a short red chiffon that had a full skirt—and I twirled before the mirror, watching it flare out around my legs.

"That's a great dress," Bernice said, "and you'll make a great entrance at the party. It's too bad you can't remember, but Loretta Young used to twirl like that when she entered a room in her TV show."

"Who's Loretta Young?"

"An actress. A beautiful Hollywood actress. Reminds me a little of you. Now don't be late. I'll have everyone there and then you'll arrive so you only have to go through one set of introductions. I'll have the door unlocked so just come right in if I don't hear you."

At precisely the right time I knocked on the door, flung it open, and did a twirl. "Hi." I must have been expected because everyone was silent, standing and staring at me. "Hi," I said again, "my name is . . ." and suddenly I couldn't remember.

I tried again. I twirled and said, "Hi, my name is . . ." I was stuck.

"Hi, Beverly," called Bernice, "come on in. Everybody, this is my friend, Beverly."

I walked into the room and made a complete circle, stopping in front of each person, extending my hand and saying, "Hi, my name is Beverly," nodding brightly as each person told me his or her name.

One guest, a fellow about my son's age, left his girl friend to walk me around the room. He seemed fascinated by everything I said.

Another guest—a young lawyer—tried to press a cigarette on me. "This will get you into the mood." Angrily, Bernice snatched the cigarette and gave it back to him. "Leave her alone," she snapped. "She's not used to this."

I didn't know why I couldn't *get* used to it. Others were smoking the cigarettes—even sharing them. Later, when Bernice walked me to my door, I asked her about this. "Oh, you poor innocent," she said. "That was grass—marijuana."

I looked at her blankly.

"It's dope, Beverly. It's no good for you. It gets you drunk in a different way and you were already pretty high on that one cocktail. I'll explain about it tomorrow. Just promise you'll not smoke the stuff. You never know what's been added to it and it can blow your mind." She laughed, "I mean even worse than yours is already blown."

"Johnny is coming to see me tomorrow night," I said happily.

"Oh, no, he's not. The nerve of him. I told him if he showed up, I'd have your husband here, waiting with a shotgun. He's got a girl friend. He's also got a wife and baby and he's a year younger than Stuart. Do you get my message?"

"I guess you mean he isn't coming."

"Correct, kid, but you sure made a great entrance."

"Did Johnny like me?"

"Yes, he liked you. But your steady boyfriend, who happens to be your husband, likes you too. Do you get the message?"

"Oh." This was a new thought. "I can only have one boyfriend at a time?"

Bernice lived around the corner, so I didn't feel afraid when Harold left after the weekend. He always left her instructions, and sometimes Shirley would come over on Thursday night to stay for the weekend, and her husband, Stan, and Hal would arrive whenever they could on Friday night. If Bernice told Harold she could not look after me that week, he would take me back with him to Cherry Hill—he was afraid to leave me unsupervised in case I got one of my crazy ideas about swimming across the ocean or running around the neighborhood.

Shirley and Stan rented the condominum and shared it casually—whoever wanted to, cooked. No one had to do anything. But Shirley was excessively neat and whenever she was there she was always cleaning or straightening up the place.

I learned about love listening to Shirley talk about her husband, Stan. He was always in her thoughts, and whenever he phoned home—just to see how she was or to tell her something about his plans—she just beamed.

When they ate in a restaurant, she watched him like a hawk. The year before, he'd had a triple bypass, and if she caught him sneaking a roll and butter, she practically snatched it out of his hand. She'd learned all about cholesteral, and put both of them on a strict diet. I thought she looked a little too thin, but evidently she loved Stan so much that she was determined to stick to their regimen. Was this love?

I had so much to learn—about people, about life . . . and especially about love.

At one of our lunches, I asked Erma if she, too, had a perfect love. "I'm always getting mad at Harold, but all of you seem so happy."

"I guess I'm happy," Erma said. "I know I'm happy. But it wasn't always like this. Don't you remember—no, you couldn't—when Bob and I broke up? It lasted about one year, and then I knew I really needed him and he knew we belonged together, too."

"You and I both felt terrible about their breakup, Bev," Shirley said. "I don't know what I'd do if it happened to me—but Stan *needs* me."

Was *this* love? Stan, it seemed, was the most important thing in Shirley's life. I thought of how casual Hal and I were about each other . . . He didn't seem worried at all about what I ate, even when I hardly touched my plate. "You're a big girl and you're studying medical things," he would say. "It's up to you to get the proper nutrition." How I yearned to have him hover over me. I envied Stan. How lucky he was to have the undivided attention of another person!

I *had* discovered romance—but not with my husband. I had a crush on my son's friend, Bill. Whenever he visited, I followed him around the house like a puppy dog. Stuart wasn't pleased. "Look, mom, you're embarrassing me. He'll think you're after him. You're old enough to be his mother."

"But he likes me, too."

"What makes you think so?"

"He told me he came to see me at the hospital."

"Oh, mom, all my friends came to see you at the hospital."

"I don't care. I like him." Oh, he was beautiful. And when he smiled at me, I glowed. One day I followed him outside and he played catch with me instead of with Stuart. Oh, my, I was proud—at last, I rated.

Then I missed the ball, and while I ran after it he laughed. I didn't like that one bit. "Why are you laughing at me?" I demanded, ready to cry.

"It's the way you run. It's so funny." More laughter.

I stalked into the house. I didn't like Bill any more. Mean and hateful boy. End of romance.

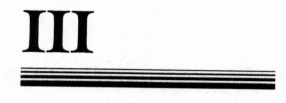

III

YOU CAN DO IT

7

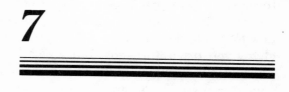

Can I Do It?

I was fascinated by my car, determined to drive. Harold said that before the accident I had driven it to work every day.

"I know I can drive," I told him. "Just show me what to do and I know I can do it."

"Do you know how dangerous it is? Do you know that if your attention strays for a second, you can have an accident?"

"I'll be good. I'll pay very good attention."

"Well, you're not ready yet. I'll show you someday."

"When? When will I be ready?" It was now July.

"I'll tell you when you're ready. Do you mind? I'm trying to read the paper."

"I'm going to drive now."

"That's nice." He wasn't paying any attention to me, safe in the knowledge that he always hid the keys. What he didn't know was that I had found his hiding place. I had watched him drive. I knew what to do. I could do it.

Harold came running out just in time to see me back the car out into the street and directly into the path of an oncoming car. Fortunately the motor had stalled. He yanked open the door, pushing me away from the wheel, and got in.

For a while he just sat there, letting off steam and scolding me. Finally, a horn honked loudly from behind and Hal pulled over to the curb and stopped. He turned and looked at me. "I don't know, Beverly. I think I'm the one going to pieces now. I just don't know how to handle you anymore. I just can't hack it. All right. I'll start giving you driving lessons, but you must not take the car out unless you're with an adult." Then he laughed ruefully. "I'm really gone. I'm sorry. You're growing up as fast as you can. I think it's my turn to need a little help."

After that, Harold started seeing a woman psychologist. But one day he said he wasn't going to her anymore. He seemed annoyed.

"I'm the one who went for therapy," he said, "but you're the one who needs a psychiatrist." It became a familiar refrain. Every time he didn't like what I was doing, he would say, "If you behave like that, you need a shrink."

"What's a shrink?"

"A psychiatrist. When you have an ego as big as yours, he shrinks it down to size."

"How do you know I have a big ego?"

"Because you think anything you want to do is so important I have to drop my work and take you. Because you think every time you run away, I'm going to rush outside after you. Need I say more?"

Another doctor—exactly what I didn't want. Especially the kind of doctor who, according to Harold, could lock you up in a mental hospital.

I devised what I thought would be a foolproof way of getting Harold off my back. I would *invent* a psychiatrist. As soon as I learned to drive, I would go to the library or art gallery—any-where—and stay away long enough so that I could come home and say I had seen my psychiatrist.

So I started "seeing" my imaginary shrink every week.

"Have a good session, hon?" Harold would ask when I came home. He was very pleased that I was getting help.

"Fine," I would say, "just fine."

I would smile mysteriously, go into the bedroom, and pretend to meditate.

When no bill came, Harold asked for this new doctor's name. Caught off guard, I gave the most outlandish name I could think of and then forgot what it was. But Harold didn't. A few days later he asked about the bill again.

"Oh," I said airily, "I'm paying for it myself."

One night when Stuart and Joanie were over for dinner, Harold brought up the subject with the kids. I was out in the kitchen, and I had to strain to hear them.

"Dad," Joanie said, "she's a little girl trying desperately to be grown-up."

"I think I'll just let it play itself out," Hal said. "She'll get tired of that game."

But it was what Stuart said that struck terror in my heart. "No, dad, I'm not just ignoring it. Since you can't find the name in the phone book, I'm calling O'Connor. I think her doctor should know."

I was hurt, bewildered, and angry. My own son was going to squeal on me! And to Dr. O'Connor, the man I wanted most to impress with what a good girl I was! Little Beverly came forward. "Tattletale, tattletale . . ."

I brought the dessert to the table, pretending I hadn't heard a word they were saying. Actually, I was relieved that they didn't ask me anything about my Dr. Whatever-his-name-was.

The fabrication quickly became a horror story, and though I realized that I had made a mistake, I didn't quite know how to get out of it. Stuart would come over to discuss my "psychiatrist" with Harold, and whenever I appeared they would change the subject.

From what I heard, Stuart had indeed told Dr. O'Connor all about my little deception, and this bolstered my suspicion that Stuart didn't like me. Why else would he have tattled on me?

One of the things I did while faking my shrink visits was to check out various religions. At the hospital, a Catholic priest had stopped in my room while making his rounds—of course I didn't know what he was at the time—and had asked me if I was Catholic.

"I don't know," I said.

He had prayed for me.

On another day a rabbi stopped by. He said he had heard that I was Jewish.

"I don't know," I said. "What's Jewish?"

He told me he hoped God would make me well soon, and left.

When I was still in the hospital, Harold had heard about these religious experiences from the nurses and had told me that I was indeed Jewish. He tried to explain that it was an old and noble religion and that on certain special days, all our family would get together in one of our homes to pray and have a special dinner.

"Oh," I said, "a party." For weeks everyone had been saying they would have a big party for me when I got well, which had been one of the reasons for the urgency in getting me home.

"No, not exactly a party, but a religious celebration."

Well, what was the difference?

I never got the special feeling that everyone else seemed to get after going to church or synagogue. The Catholic church surprised me. Why did people have to get down on their knees to talk to God? Couldn't he hear if you were in bed, or sitting at the kitchen table? I thought He went by mental telepathy, the way the gray-haired lady did.

Once I'd decided that religion wasn't for me, I wondered if a job would be the answer. Maybe working would prove to everybody that I was okay, that I didn't need a psychiatrist.

My mother didn't understand.

"Why do you want a job? You have a husband, and he can look after you. You worked enough years already."

"Is that what a husband is?" I asked. "The man who looks after you? Is that why you have a husband?"

"It used to be. But in my case, I ended up working in the store shoulder to shoulder with your father—ask him."

"She's right," dad said. "Your grandmother took care of you, and mama worked in the grocery store with me."

"Did I work when I had babies?" I asked.

"Did you ever," said my mother. "Your cousin, Shirley, wasn't working—her husband was a big jeweler—so she took care of Stuart. And when Joanie started school, Joanie would come home to Shirley instead of to you and you would pick her up on the way home from work. Ask Shirley. That's why I say you should be very nice to your cousin. She was always your best friend and now you don't pay much attention to her."

"I don't know her," I said. "But I'm trying to know her now."

"She thinks you maybe remember her a little. Stick with her, Beverly, maybe she can help you remember."

I was so tired of people trying to make me remember.

"Tell me again about my jobs, mama. Tell me about that."

"Well, I've told you. You were very smart. We sent you for a year to the university so you could study how to be an assistant to a doctor or dentist. We were very proud of you. You got a good job with one of the finest dentists."

Later I talked to Harold about whether he thought I could get a job with a dentist now.

"No, I don't think so. It's pretty complicated work."

"What did I do for the dentist?"

"A lot of things."

"Did I clean teeth?"

He was sure I had because I had talked of it at home—"But only children's. He straightened children's teeth."

"I know. Orthodontist."

"You've got it. Good girl."

"What do you think I am? A dummy?"

"Your favorite word."

"No, it's not. My favorite word is *smart*. No, my favorite word is *knowing*. Knowing is such a good feeling. You know how they say 'Happiness is a warm kitten,' or something like that? Well, to me happiness is *knowing*. I wish I could tell you what a good feeling knowing is, and not being a dummy."

"Your favorite word again."

"Oh, shut up."

Now he looked angry. "You're not supposed to say that. It's a no-no."

"It's not cussing. I can say it if it's not cussing."

"I give up."

"Ha, ha, who's the dummy?"

Even when we had company—maybe *especially* when we had company—I would take every opportunity to show off my new learning. "Oh," I would say, "I'm reading about the heart," and I would open the book to the chapter on the heart and say, "Do you want to ask me anything about the heart?"

Harold would look at the guests with his apologetic I-have-to-humor-her look," and say "Yeah, Bev, what's in the heart?"

Now the stage was set . . . I would begin my recitation. "Well, there's the atrium and the ventricle and one is the top part and one is the bottom . . . And when the venous blood enters from the right atrium. . ." By the time I had gotten the blood safely into the pulmonary artery everyone would be looking at me with glazed eyes of boredom, but I didn't care. I was the teacher!

Hal would always interrupt me.

"That's just fine, Beverly—isn't it, folks?"

"Oh, yes," they would say. "Are you studying to be a nurse now?"

"No, I'm going to teach like Harold says I used to."

They would look at each other sadly and murmur something encouraging.

"You'll see," I'd say. "I can do it. I've studied all about the lungs, too. Do you want to hear?"

"Sure, but later. Aren't you going to eat something?"

"Oh yes. I forgot." But it was always clear to everyone that I would have much preferred continuing my lecture. Their praise was *my* nourishment—and I savored every morsel.

Slowly I was changing, and the day came when I wasn't swearing anymore. Hal noticed. "What's the matter, Beverly? You're not cussing me today."

"Should I? Do you want me to?"

"That's a joke, Bev. I was just making a joke."

"What's a joke?"

"That's when you say one thing and mean another. It's supposed to make you laugh. Ha, ha."

There was still so much to learn!

People would say that Harold should have become a comedian, that he had a way with words. I thought they were lucky they weren't on the receiving end of his funny words. One night, over dinner with Shirley and Erma, when we were all trying to remember a particular anniversary date, Harold said, "Do you remember FDR? Do you remember his Day of Infamy speech?"

"He means when the Japanese declared war on us and bombed Pearl Harbor," Shirley explained, seeing my blank expression. "What date are you talking about? Oh, he means December seventh—Pearl Harbor Day."

"Wrong!" said Hal. "I'm talking about March eleventh."

"But that isn't Pearl Harbor Day," said Shirley.

"Of course not," Harold said, straight-faced. "That's our wedding day—*my* day of infamy." Everyone howled with laughter and looked at me. I sat perfectly still, trying to summon up a chuckle.

I wanted to stay a child. I wished I could live in my granddaughter Aryn's world, but the adults wouldn't let me. I was supposed to learn to act like them. If I wanted to go to a restaurant, if I wanted to go visiting, if I wanted almost anything, I had to straighten up and act like a grown-up lady. I was now an almost forty-nine-year-old-woman, and I was acting like my four-year-old granddaughter.

"I feel like a four-year-old," I told Harold. "Why is that bad?"

"It's not *bad*," he said, "it's just inappropriate behavior, to quote Dr. O'Connor, as well as Dr. LaFlare. Now will you believe me?"

Shirley and Erma kept taking me to lunches and treating me like an adult. But if I'd had my choice, I would have been on the floor with Aryn and her little friends. Unfortunately, my preference wasn't exactly reciprocated. While my granddaughter was tolerant of me, her friends weren't. Sometimes they appealed to Joanie. "Make grandma quit bothering us. We don't want her to play with us anymore today."

"Okay, grandma," Joanie would say. "Your time is up. You can play with them again tomorow. Right, children?"

"Sure, okay." Anything to get rid of the big nuisance, at least for the moment.

But Shirley and Erma ignored my childish prattle and continued to tell me about what was going on in their world. Their problems, their husbands' problems. Stan and Bob, partners in a jewelry store, were thinking of dissolving the partnership—something about the economy being down. I knew Harold had job problems too, but I wasn't particularly interested—I gathered the problem had something to do with his not getting paid and having to do certain jobs over.

"What do you have to do over again?" I asked for the tenth time.

"The siding. The goddamn house siding on the area around the entry. They changed their mind and they're blaming it on me." He seemed all excited. I didn't get it—so what if he had to do it over?

I did many pages of writing over and over too, copying a book, didn't I?

"I do it over, too."

"You're studying, kid. I'm talking about hard labor and losing the profit of a job."

Profit. That meant money. "Is that why you told Erma I can't buy anything anymore?"

"Well, that's part of it. You just can't buy everything in sight that strikes your fancy. I'm not made of money."

He had a point. I had already learned how to say the magic word "Layaway," and Harold had finally found it necessary to have Erma put on the restraints.

And it was Erma who stepped in to orchestrate the color coordination of my new wardrobe when my partiality for bright colors threatened to make me look like a clown. If I'd had my way, I would have worn red shoes with a yellow hat, a green dress, and a blue handbag.

Weeks passed. I was changing every day. Now, when there were grown-ups around, I would sit by and watch the children play, playing along with them only in my head. Something told me Little Bevie was in danger, so now I only let her come out every once in a while. By protecting her, I was protecting myself. Couldn't people understand that?

July 1980, just a few months after I had left the hospital, I went with Harold to the lawyer's office to sign some papers for the insurance adjustment. I was not particularly curious or excited about this venture, but I went along with it. The amount was $19,000—not exactly a fortune, Harold said, given the fact that the accident had ruined my life and possibly cut my earning power to zero.

"But I'm going to go to work again," I said.

Harold gave me his old skeptical look.

"Don't count on it and raise your hopes too high. What work could you do? There's a lot you have to know first."

"Don't worry. I can do it. I'm studying real hard."

"Come now, Beverly, be honest. What are you studying?"

"I'm studying my medical books. I'm going to be a teacher again." I was getting angry. "You just think I'm a dummy. You'll see."

"I'm sure you can do it, honey. Just don't rush it. Take it easy. Meanwhile, the nineteen thousand dollars will help us get a start in business. I'd like to be an owner for a change. I'm tired of someone else telling me what to do."

"So am I," I said. "You're always telling me what to do. I want to be my own boss."

"Okay, I'll let you tell me what to do. Say, aren't you going to ask me what business I'm going into?"

"No."

"Well, you have the right to know. Remember Butch? No, you wouldn't remember Butch. He came to dinner a couple times in the old days. I ran into him and happened to tell him about you and the insurance, and he said he wouldn't mind expanding his home repair business—taking in a partner."

"That's nice. Who's the partner?"

He looked disgusted.

"Me, of course. How can you get a job if you don't catch on to things!"

"I *did* know. I did understand. I just wanted you to say it. You said not to jump on people's lines and to let them finish their own sentences."

"Okay, dear. I understand. So anyway, I'm going to be his partner and I'll work my own hours, and I can spend more time with you and my money will work for me."

"How will it do that?" It was a quaint thought—*money* working.

"Because I'll get a cut on all work brought in by other salesmen."

"Oh."

At the lawyer's office I listened to Hal and the lawyer. Apparently the driver of the car that had struck me didn't have much insurance, and this was the best settlement we could get. Briefly, Harold talked to the lawyer about the possibility of suing, but then he decided that it was probably better to settle for the bird in the hand and be done with it.

I didn't see a bird anywhere and made a note in my little pad to ask about that. Later, Harold explained about how hard it is to chase after birds you see in a bush and how you might lose hold of the bird you have in your hand if you decide to chase after the others. "Birds, money—it's the same thing. Lots of times you talk about one thing, but you mean another."

"I know," I said, "that's poetry. You talk about one thing and you mean another. I've been reading about that at the library. And you use it in wise old sayings like 'Birds of a feather flock together,' and that can mean criminals flock together."

"Bravo, Bev. You're getting there."

I was much more interested in his praise than in my $19,000. "And they say 'She's a bird,' and that means she's acting crazy and that's not good but if they say, 'She's a songbird,' that's a compliment because it means she's a great singer . . ."

"Or a great tattletale, ratting on her friends."

" . . . and then there's a title of a book, *Sweet Bird of Youth,* and the bird means being young . . ."

"Hold on, Bev. Slow down. I think it's a play by Tennessee Williams and not a book, but it doesn't matter. I'm so pleased with the way your mind is picking things up. But now can we just change the subject from birds?"

I was happy to—I'd just about run out of thoughts on the subject, except that I wanted to tell him again about how I had tried to pet the birds on the neighbor's lawn and could not understand why they had avoided me and flown away. As I pondered the way of the world, those birds often came to mind. To make a bird stay, you had to bribe it with food. Did you have to do that with people, too?

For a moment—but only a moment—I wondered if that was what my $19,000 was—a bribe to a man. There was something there I couldn't quite reach. I let it go.

With the $19,000 check safely in Harold's pocket, he suggested we go to a nice restaurant and celebrate.

That was fine with me. I could look at the pretty people and talk to them. I didn't bother telling them about the $19,000 check in my husband's pocket. It wasn't that important.

Getting a job became the most important thing in my life. I was making progress, I knew it. It had started out, more or less, as a way to impress Harold. He would come home and find me lying on my stomach or sitting on the floor with my array of books scattered around me. I would be filling a tablet with medical jargon, none of it making any sense. I was sure that this would impress Harold and put to rest any thoughts that I should be back in the hospital.

Eventually, I was copying whole pages from the books and Harold would find me sitting at the table surrounded by my books and ballpoint pens and pencils. I had discovered colored felt tips and would change colors every paragraph. Gradually it started to make a little sense and the writing came more easily. Harold put a dictionary on the table and showed me how to look up words.

By August, I felt totally wise. I was all right now, I was sure. It was some kind of miracle. A cloud had lifted. I knew so much. The books made sense. Good sense. I was ready for a job. I knew it. Before, I had only been bragging—and hoping. Now I had a sure feeling inside.

Harold didn't think so, but how could he know? He couldn't see inside my head. All he would say was, "We'll see."

I had to prove it with a job. *That* would convince him.

It became an obsession. I had to show the world I wasn't a dummy, that I didn't need psychiatric help. I scoured the papers' want-ad sections and made Harold take me on countless futile interviews for medical jobs for which I was totally unsuited. He never wanted to be seen with me on these jaunts, so he would wait for me in the lobby or out in the car.

The interview usually ended with, "We'll let you know." Of course they rarely did, and I always ended up in tears.

"If you're going to carry on like that," Harold would say, "then you *are* a dummy! Don't you realize it takes time? Don't you realize you aren't ready yet? You don't know the words." But I desperately wanted to feel important, to feel needed.

I loved being a helper. Whenever we were invited to someone's house, I would say brightly, "Let me help," and I would bustle around the kitchen as if it were my own. I would ask people if they wanted more of this or that and jump up from the table to get it.

Things came to a head one day at a gathering at Joanie's house. I was being my usual helpful self, running in and out of the kitchen, when Harold called from the living room. "Bev, come here."

I hurried over. "What can I get you?"

"I want you to sit down here with me."

"I can't, I'm helping." I ran back into the kitchen.

Harold was strangely silent on the ride home. "Why are you mad at me?" I burst out when we arrived home. "What dummy thing did I do?"

"You didn't do anything wrong. You were trying to be nice."

"Then why are you mad?"

"I'm not mad. I'm disgusted. Come to the kitchen and let's have a cup of coffee."

Uh-oh. I followed him, dreading whatever was to come.

"Beverly, whose house were we in?"

"Joanie's."

"Whose party was it?"

"Joanie's and Steve's."

"Did Joanie ask you to help her?"

"No."

"Was anyone else running in and out of the kitchen—any other guest, I mean?"

"No."

"Were the other women all sitting with their husbands?"

"Yes, except Joanie."

"Right. It was Joanie's party. And do you know who you are?"

"Who?"

"You're the matriarch of the family when you're with your daughter and her husband and their children. And a matriarch is the honored guest, and she is older and dignified. The younger ladies get her what *she* wants. She doesn't act like the maid. And especially when her husband is there and wants her to sit with him and be a guest."

"But I like helping her. I like to help."

"Did you ever stop to think she might want to do it her way?"

"All she has to do is tell me."

"Exactly. Why don't you tell Joanie or whoever your hostess is to come get you if you can be of help."

"What if she doesn't ask me?"

"Let's hope she doesn't. Then you can be a guest like the rest of the guests. You don't have to work for your supper."

"I don't know what to talk about."

"Just keep reading the newspapers and all your books and when subjects come up, you'll think of something to say. Nobody expects you to sound like a professor already. Just enjoy listening to what they're saying. You're doing fine. You're catching on to lots of things. I'm proud of you. Your progress."

"No, you're not. You're ashamed of me."

"Come on now, would I want you to come sit beside me if I weren't proud of you?"

"I don't know."

"Okay, dummy, now you know—I *want* you there beside me."

I felt very good inside. Somehow, when he said it that way, he didn't mean *dummy*.

———————————

"It was increasingly becoming my impression that, aside from any psychosocial problems which this woman might have and which have resulted in her total amnesia for all of her life prior to the automobile accident, she is also compromised organically. Certainly her behavior does suggest some frontal lobe damage—her childlike interest in things, the inappropriateness of the way in which she approaches strangers and talks with them. I might add that, after I had seen her husband and we walked down to the waiting room, she was perched on the windowsill, looking out at a squirrel playing on the ground, was quite oblivious to the fact that we had walked into the room, and was laughing to herself with childlike pleasure at what she had seen."

8

Happiness Is a Three-letter Word

A job, a job, my kingdom for a job!

I looked at the books that proved I had once been a teacher.

I looked at my books on dentistry. Every tooth had a name, every tooth had a number. I memorized them. It was surprising how much a dentist had to know about medicine, pain killers, side effects, bleeding and blood vessels, office emergencies—fear, fainting, screaming.

There was a solution for everything. I had worked for an orthodontist for eleven years. Had I helped him through many emergencies? I would probably never know.

I bombarded Harold with questions—many of which he couldn't answer—about my teaching jobs. "You have a neighbor— Evelyn Portnoy—who used to teach with you," he said. "Don't you remember? She came to see you and you were barely polite. She tried to tell you about your past jobs. I was hoping that seeing her would bring back your past."

"Oh, good," I said. "I sort of remember her now. I want to talk to her. I want to talk to her right now. I'll listen."

I was fascinated by Evelyn's story. Apparently I had even helped *her* get jobs. She had been my friend, and every time I had made a change, I would insist that she teach at the same place. Until my last job—I had just switched to Philadelphia Training School when the accident happened.

Maybe if she had been with me when I crossed that street, the accident would never have happened and I would still be that other Beverly. It was a shocking thought. Evelyn was still at Lyons Institute, teaching, when I had moved on. Maybe it was fate that she had decided to sit this move out.

I couldn't believe I had had *five* teaching jobs. Evidently I had been very ambitious, very career-oriented, and was searching for the perfect private school and best advancement. I had to teach in a private school because I had not finished college and had no teaching degree. I was hired on the basis of my experience.

"Why did I go into teaching if I had a good job already as assistant to a dentist?"

"You told me you didn't want to be a girl friday forever," Evelyn said. "You were the only woman in the dentist's office and you had to be the all-round helper—secretary and assistant. You thought it would be a step up to teach others, and you had big dreams of the future. And you could have long summer vacations. School holidays."

"Sounds good. How did I get my first job?"

Evelyn didn't know—but it had been at the Delaware Valley Training School.

Her eye fell on a little kit I had found in a plastic case with "The Tooth Game" printed on it.

"That was ours," she said. "The Tooth Game was ours."

"What do you mean, *ours?* We used it to teach, didn't we?"

"Yes, but we invented it, too. But since we were working for American Services, they told us they were taking out a copyright on it. See?"

I looked and the game did indeed have a *c* for copyright on the front of it along with the name, "The Tooth Game," and the logo for the American Services Company.

"Boy, we were mad. Do you know what we did?"

"What? Cuss at the boss?"

"And lose our jobs? Don't be silly. We invented a second game to patent or copyright under our own names and it was for children, for parents to buy their children, and we were going to call it 'The Tooth Fairy Game.' "

I was thrilled.

"Oh, do we have a patent?"

"No, I don't know what happened. I have a copy of the letter we sent the patent office, but then we sort of lost interest. But we could still do it. Hey, maybe we'll do it."

"Sure. That would be fun. Why didn't we keep on with it?"

"I guess we were so busy changing jobs and keeping up with other things. We sure had a lot of laughs. You know what they called us? Frick and Frack." Evelyn was laughing.

"What does that mean?" I laughed too, but I was wondering if we should feel insulted.

"We never found out. I guess we didn't ask. We thought it was some vaudeville or burlesque team before our time."

I wished I could remember something funny from those days.

"I can give you the perfect illustration," Evelyn said. "There was a man we couldn't stand because he was very bossy. I mean, even *we* didn't like him and we liked just about everyone. And did he have an ego! Oh, my. And he thought we didn't know that he was wearing a hairpiece."

"Did other people know he was wearing one?"

"I don't know. To show you his ego, he had three wigs and he would wear them in sequence to show that his hair was growing out."

"I don't believe it."

"Believe it. And number three wig was shaggy like 'Oh, boy, do I need a haircut.' So one day there was a neighborhood meeting on some problem and he was standing up ranting and raving and telling everyone what they had to do and in his excitement he waved his glasses around and tapped his head so hard, he tilted his hairpiece and it sat there lopsided."

We both laughed. "What happened?" I asked. "Did he find out?"

"Probably not till he got home. But all the rest of that meeting we didn't hear a word of what he was saying. We sat there pretending to be listening and all we could do is choke back the laughter. I think he gave us a dirty look."

I couldn't believe my eyes when I visited Evelyn's home down the street. She had needlepoint pictures all over the living room, the dining room, the family room, and even the kitchen. "Of course I have them," she said. "We used to do needlepoint together."

I was amazed at all the Oriental things Evelyn had in her living room, especially a little Japanese doll under a huge glass bell. "I guess this doll is very precious to you, Evelyn."

"Oh, yes. I love it. But you loved the Oriental look, too."

There was that word *love* again. Everyone loved something.

I didn't love my Oriental things anymore. What did I love? My books. My medical books, which showed the deep understanding of technical things that I'd once had.

I kept carrying my books back and forth to Atlantic City, poring over them whenever the mood struck, which was often. I even took them with me across the street to the beach. Sometimes Bernice, who often joined me on the beach, wouldn't know the meaning of a word and I would be surprised that someone so wise didn't know something I knew.

Another neighbor, Ruth, a travel agent, would go to the beach with us and talk about far-off places. It thrilled me. I hadn't quite accepted the fact that the whole world wasn't Cherry Hill and Philadelphia, and I was full of questions.

Bernice believed that I would go back to work. One day Ruth said, "Bernice, you get around. Why don't you see if she could get some kind of simple job to get her feet wet? To heck with the future. She could work now."

I pretended I was reading, but my heart leaped. I had a goal and *someone* had faith in me. A new adventure!

As the days went by, I learned some surprising things about myself and my career from Evelyn. Me, little me, had gone to schools to speak to senior high school classes about becoming medical and dental assistants and secretaries. Certain schools would even request me. Who knew how many careers I had influenced?

"Do you know you got me started as a teacher, too?" Evelyn asked.

"I did?" I was delighted to take credit for something.

"You sure did. I was a dental assistant here in Cherry Hill after you had switched to teaching. We were both new on our street, since they were just building the houses on Brandywood Drive. Everybody was talking to everybody else and getting acquainted, being neighborly. We were so happy to find we were in the same field—both dental assistants—and we just hit it off."

"I didn't know that. I'm so glad I had a friend."

"You sure did, honey. As a matter of fact, I was so impressed with what you told me about teaching that I thought maybe I could follow in your footsteps. Anyway, when you switched schools and moved to your third school, McCarrie, and came and told me there was another opening, you didn't have much trouble pushing me into it."

"I did that?"

"Yes. You were a very loyal friend. You wanted me with you and you convinced me I could do it, even though I had no degree in teaching. You said I could do it. You were like the pied piper because when you moved to American Training and set up their new school for medical and dental assistant training, you got me to quit and be one of your teachers. You were the supervisor of the school."

"I was? Well, la-di-dah, I was Madame Big, wasn't I?"

"Darn right. And then when that company folded and you got a job at Lyons Institute, you insisted I come there too."

"I got you a job?"

"You were working it out behind the scenes and I'm still there. I felt terrible when you went to Philadelphia Training and had the accident—maybe if I'd been there . . ."

"I know. But at least now I know you and you can tell me what I used to be like."

There was a moment of silence. To lighten things, Evelyn introduced me to her two cats—Cleopatra and C.J., or Con Job. "I'm a pack rat. Wait a minute. I'm going to show you a picture in the newspaper of both of us in front of one of our schools. Oh sure, we were famous among our friends—Frick and Frack at work." She laughed and, leaving the room for a few minutes, returned with a long article entitled "School Trains Paradentals—Aides Learn Dentistry in Pilot Program."

In it there was a big picture of both of us in white uniforms standing in front of the school's sign, "AMERICAN TRAINING SERVICES—PARAMEDICAL."

I couldn't believe I had worn my hair so short. It looked like a boy's haircut. "You told me you used to go to the beauty parlor for permanents," Evelyn said, "but you said you didn't have time for that foolishness anymore and you just wanted it to be practical. You'd have it whacked off once in a while."

"That's not like me now," I said. "I like my curls and I like my hair grown out."

"And that new color is a lot peppier than the old Beverly would have worn."

"I know. I like really red hair and I'm going to wear it from now on." I read the article about the new paramedical school. Evidently we both had been in on the ground floor in the teaching of paradentals, although my title was supervisory instructor. Students were taught to assist dentists by taking x-rays, preparing materials needed for tooth impressions, preparing the patient in a treatment room before the dentist entered, doing lab work and even billing and simple bookkeeping.

Evelyn and I had been very busy, getting the courses set up for the first group of students and working on the Tooth Game. The caption of the picture was "Waiting for completion" and went on to say that the new school was located in the New Albany Medical Clinic in Cinnaminson.

After the paradental school was on its feet, the paramedical section was due to open. I became supervisor of that division. The main teacher of paramedics, Evelyn said, was a registered nurse. I liked the thought that *I* had once had supervision over a nurse. I must not have been a dummy after all.

And I liked the fact that I had gone out of my way to help students get jobs when they were through with their training.

I had been almost a workaholic, Evelyn said—deeply involved in my career, very concerned about the education of my children, a demon housekeeper, caught up in a whirl of parties and dinners with Shirley and Erma and all our husbands, involved in civic affairs—"And," she added, "you attacked tennis as if your life depended on it."

That certainly wasn't me. That was the Other Image. Hearing all she had done, the paragon of virtue that she had been, I almost resented her.

It was my friend Bernice who got the new Beverly her first job— or at least pointed her in the right direction. Bernice knew a woman lawyer who was the director of the Camden County Consumer Affairs Office and who needed someone to investigate consumer complaints.

"It's just what you like, Bev," Bernice told me. "Talking to people."

"Yes," I said, "I love to talk to people."

"And listening to their complaints."

"About what?" I asked.

"About any situation in which they feel someone cheated or took advantage of them. You have to look into it and try to straighten it out. Decide who's right and who's wrong. Do you think you could do that?"

"Of course. But give me an example of who would cheat them."

"It could be anyone. It could be a store that charged double or that won't take back merchandise that isn't good. Or a doctor or dentist who's gouging someone. Maybe a dentist made a set of false teeth that don't fit and he still demands his money."

"Oh, I could handle that. I would talk to both sides and I would find out the truth."

"Of course you would. Call this woman—Barbara Berman—and make an appointment with her. She lives in Cherry Hill, too. You can give me as a reference."

"When I applied for other jobs I could give only Shirley and Erma as references—now I can give all three names!" I was thrilled.

On the way to the interview, Harold was his usual pessimistic self. "Don't get your hopes up. You're not ready yet, and they can see it."

"How can they see it?"

"You aren't tactful with people. You just tell them bluntly what you think." Tact. That was exactly what Bernice had warned me about. But I knew tact now. I was sure I did.

"No, no. You taught me tact, Harold. Now I can handle it."

"Well, it doesn't matter because you won't get the job anyway."

But I *did*—over three other applicants, too! Miss Berman told me that I was to start on Monday. Harold's mouth flew open when I told him. "You must be kidding. Well, you may be ready if you listen to me. Don't ever tell anyone, 'You're wrong, you're wrong,' the way you do around here, and for Christ's sake, no cussing."

"Okay. I'll remember that. But if I don't say, 'You're wrong,' what do I say?"

"Say, 'I believe you've made a mistake.' Or, 'Your defense is not sound,' or, 'I find the evidence is stronger on the store's side and they have fulfilled their obligation to you.' "

"So I'm sorry, I cannot ask them to refund your money," I finished.

"Hey, Bev, that's great. Really tactful. You can do it."

"I told you I can do it." But just to be sure, Hal made up

complaints and took one side or the other, being nasty and unreasonable, while I tried to remain firm and tactful. He was pleased with my progress.

"You've come a long way from Graduate Hospital, baby."

On my first day I felt very strong and secure as I listened to my instructions. Miss Berman was not nearly as tough as Harold, and she assured me that she understood about my amnesia and that I could come to her as often as needed until I got adjusted to my new job. People would be calling in, and I was to explain that their complaints must be sent in writing. Once I received the written complaints, I would send them a form to fill out, which would become part of the office files. I would be called an investigator. *My* decision would be final.

Every Monday, a conference was held and cases were assigned to us. The man who knew all about cars and trucks was to hear all the dealer complaints. I was given mostly medical cases and store complaints.

My first case involved a furniture store that was demanding the balance of payment for rugs that a customer, a blind man, said were never delivered. I went to the man's house; there were no rugs. I went to the warehouse and asked to see delivery records. There was nothing with his signature on it. The store had insisted that the customer had received the goods, but could not prove this. In two weeks I got them to deliver and install the rugs.

I was excited about other cases I was working on, too. A hospital had sent a bill for several thousand dollars to a sixty-two-year-old man who had entered as an emergency patient with symptoms of a heart attack. According to the complainant, the hospital had done nothing for him except to put him in a room and give him an I.V. Occasionally a doctor had stopped in just to ask how he was doing, and subsequently charged a hefty consultation fee. After a week, the patient had finally gotten dressed and walked out.

I looked at the hospital records. There was no evidence that the patient had even received an EKG. The hospital administrator was of no help—all he did was repeat that the man would have to pay his bill.

I struggled to be tactful but I was angry. I went to the Health Association of the State of New Jersey; more discussions followed at the hospital. Finally it was decided that the patient should pay only for the room. All service charges were dropped. The poor man was so grateful that he and his wife came to thank me in person.

The there was the case of the young girl who had enrolled in a private trade school to learn to be a medical secretary. She had paid $2,000 of the full $2,400 fee, but disgusted with the poor quality of the training she was getting, she had refused to pay the last $400 shortly before graduation.

The school said she could not graduate and refused to give her the certificate she needed to get a job even though she had passed all tests and her attendance had been perfect.

When the girl was told she would not graduate, she changed her mind and promised that she would pay the $400 as soon as she had a job. But the school was adamant, saying she would have to attend school an extra three months and still pay the $400 before graduation. That's when she came to us for help.

I went to the school and told them I felt they were wrong in their treatment of the girl—tact, tact, I reminded myself—but they said their decision was final. I talked to them a second time and said that if they did not let the girl graduate and pay later, she would probably take the matter to court.

"Fine," said the haughty school official, "go to court." Without consulting anyone back at the office I marched the girl directly from the school office to the nearby courthouse and started the court case. Papers were served on the school and six weeks later we were in court. I didn't have to testify, and I was as happy as my client when the court decided that the school had to give her her certificate and she was not required to go to school an additional three months. She was assured she could finish paying the tuition after she got her first job.

But I was not always on the side of the complainant. Once a woman came to us wanting her money back for a seventy-five-dollar eye examination. Her argument was that the man who had administered the exam was only an optometrist, that he had charged too much, that he had not spent enough time with her, and that he had not actually fitted her with glasses, but had only given her a prescription.

"Did you ask in advance what he charged?" I asked.

"No."

I went to see the optometrist. Eventually I reported back to the woman that I did not find any evidence to indicate that the optometrist had treated her any differently from his other patients. He was a licensed optometrist and he had done exactly what he was licensed to do—give her a prescription. I told her that the length of time spent with a patient varies from doctor to doctor. "And I saw his books," I added. "That's what he charges."

"But what about the price?" she said. "I think seventy-five dollars is outrageous."

"You had the right to ask his price before the examination. But as a matter of fact, that was within the range of what other optometrists in that area charge."

She pounced on that. "Aha, how do you know what they charge? How did you check?"

"I know because I went into their offices and pretended to be a patient and asked what they charged. From sixty-five to seventy-five dollars seemed to be standard."

"Oh," she said, chastened. "Well, what do you think I should do?"

"I think you should get your prescription filled and just chalk it up to experience. Now you know that education is expensive."

I was completely engrossed in my job and proud to be doing adult work. But now I had another adult challenge—I wanted to have a surprise birthday party for Harold. His birthday was in the latter part of February and I was hoping that preparing for a party would distract me from the fact that February thirteenth—the first anniversary of my accident—was approaching.

I chose Super Bowl Day for the celebration and sent out "*Supper* Bowl" invitations. It would be a buffet and everyone could eat while watching the Philadelphia Eagles take on the Oakland Raiders.

It was Joanie who had found me floundering in the kitchen, trying to make icing for the two cakes that had suddenly gone lopsided on their way out of the oven. "I don't know what happened to them," I said. "They just collapsed on one side."

My icing wasn't anything to write home about, either.

"Well, don't worry about it," she laughed. "We've got a lot of other things to do. I'll take care of the cake tonight. The party is tomorrow, you know."

I was terrified.

Thirty people were coming. Inviting them was one thing, but

the reality of actually having them there was quite another. Nothing was ready. Fortunately, Joanie had taken charge. All the food was stored at her house, and my only job—not counting the unfortunate cakes—was to get Harold out of the house the next day while she set tables and got the buffet ready. It wasn't easy.

I finally had to resort to one of my tantrums. I told Harold I had to go shopping, it was an emergency, and he had to come with me because I couldn't bear to be alone.

"Oh, Lord, how long?" he groaned as he followed me out the door. I promised to get him back in time for his precious game.

"That's not what I was talking about—" he said. "I thought you had outgrown this phase."

When we got back at three, everyone jumped up and yelled, "Happy Birthday."

He looked as if *he* had lost his memory.

Joanie had finally given up on my fiasco and had picked up a birthday cake at the bakery. The food was fine—everything I had made as well as Joanie's contributions. But what amazed the guests were the games I had chosen for them to play after the Super Bowl . . . Pin the Tail on the Donkey and Hide and Seek!

Most of them humored me. Later I learned that such games were only played at children's birthday parties. Well, what could you expect when I had gotten my information on birthday parties from my four-year-old-going-on-five granddaughter?

This was a happy time. I had a job I loved, a family I was learning to love again . . . How was I to know that just a few weeks later, my lovely world would come to a grinding halt?

One morning Miss Berman called me into her office. Evidently there was budget trouble and some jobs would have to be eliminated. I had been the last one hired and so I was going to have to be the first one fired.

I was almost in tears.

"What kind of rule is that? Wasn't I doing a good job?"

She assured me over and over that there was nothing wrong with my performance and that she had gotten good reports about me, but I left her office convinced that there must have been something wrong with the way I was doing the job.

Even when Miss Berman herself left the company to go back to her private law practice, I believed I had somehow failed to measure up.

I went back to my books. I bought two medical dictionaries and kept them at my side at all times.

I would sit at the table, reading my lists aloud: "in-frac-tion, in-fra-red, in-fric-tion, in-fun-dib-u-lum, in-fu-sion, in-ges-ta, in-gra-ves-cent, in-gre-di-ent, in-gui-nal."

"At least I know *ingredient*," said Hal. "What's that one mean with the 'fun' in it?"

"In-fun-dib-u-lum," I read. "That means a passageway in the body that is funnel-shaped."

"Oh, heck," he said. "No fun *there*."

The real little Bev at four years old

Hal and his girl—is that really me?—on their wedding day, March 11, 1951

"I do."

The old Bev and Harold at Joan's confirmation in 1967

Stuart hamming it up on the beach in Ventnor, N.J., 1966

Joanie was always very close to her dad

Joanie and Stuart

My parents, Harry and Ann Kaufman

The women in my life

Stuart and Mari honeymooning in Hawaii

"The Group"

A pensive moment by my favorite silk flowers

With my grown-up son, Stuart

Shirley and Bev in their Atlantic City apartment

The new Bev

IV

SEARCH FOR A PAST— A DETECTIVE STORY

9

Sleeping Beauty

I felt like Sleeping Beauty waiting for her prince. Everyone, it seemed, had a different theory of how to wake me up and bring back my memory.

My parents thought stories of my childhood would do it. Joanie thought time would do it. Stuart seemed to think I had actually regained my memory but was just not telling. He kept trying to trick me into admitting I did remember. *That* hurt.

Erma and Shirley thought that seeing my first house in Philadelphia would do it. I had raised my children there. Erma had been a close neighbor. My beloved dog Loco had lived and died there.

As Erma and I drove through Mount Airy, I felt glad that I didn't live there anymore. We passed her old street and then stopped the car in front of a row of houses, all attached, each one looking exactly like the other. "Which one?" I asked.

"That one," she pointed as we got out of the car. I stood at the front lawn, feeling nothing. I walked up and down the sidewalk, trying to summon up a memory or a feeling. Nothing. I walked up to the door. Still, nothing came.

"You used to sit out here and read," she said, indicating the chairs in front of the house. "They may even be the same chairs, but I don't know. It's not Cherry Hill, you can see."

I stood there, frowning.

"I didn't know you could have a patio in front of a house. That isn't right. Don't you have to have a patio in back of a house?"

"I really don't know the exact meaning of the word—it's Spanish. Look it up."

"I will." I wrote it down in my ever-present little notebook. I didn't want to hang around here—this place wasn't mine. Some other person had lived here and I was glad it wasn't me.

On the way out of town, Erma drove slowly past the stores I had gone shopping in almost every day of my life. Nothing. *Poor little house*, I thought. *Poor little town.*

Erma could see that I was sad. She patted my hand. "I'm so sorry it didn't work. I was so sure it would that I didn't even want you to be alone when you came here for fear you would panic when you recognized it." Dear Erma.

"Don't forget to look up *patio*," she said as she let me off in front of my house.

My trusty dictionary defined *patio* as a courtyard. So I looked up *courtyard*. That night I had a little surprise for Harold. Now we would see who was smart and who was dumb. What did *he* call that thing we sat on outside?

"A patio," he said. Aha! He'd swallowed the bait . . .

"Wrong," I said, triumphantly, and proceeded to explain with a superior air that a patio was an uncovered area in the middle of a house or surrounded by walls. "It's a courtyard," I said, holding up the dictionary.

He was *not* amused.

"I don't care what the dictionary says. There is no other name. What would you call that thing in back?"

"Cement in the ground."

He smiled.

"I rest my case," I said triumphantly.

One day, out of the blue I said to Hal, "I'm not supposed to sleep in a little bed and you're not supposed to sleep in a little bed."

He looked surprised.

"I'm not? What makes you say that?"

"There's one *big* bed somewhere."

"There is? Tell me where."

"I don't know." Distracted, I walked into the kitchen to fix dinner.

He followed me.

"Tell me again what you said about the big bed. It's very important to me."

"I didn't say anything."

"Yes, you did. You said you and I weren't supposed to sleep in 'little beds,' meaning, I'm sure, twin beds. Tell me again."

I didn't know why he seemed so excited. "I don't know, Harold. I didn't say anything." Often I still forgot what I had just been talking about.

"Beverly," he shook me, "think hard. Do you remember when we used to sleep in a big bed?"

"No. Did we?"

"Yes. But I was so restless, we ended up getting twin beds."

"We did?"

"Yes, I would get up in the middle of the night and pace and read awhile. Do you remember that?"

"No."

"Well, honey, then I think you had another one of those flutters or flashes. Like the dressmaker you can't remember. You remember for an instant and it's gone. Your memory is flickering. Maybe it will come on like an electric light one day—very strong." Happily, he hugged me.

I was puzzled. Why couldn't these little pieces of the puzzle stay remembered?

Harold shrugged.

"Doctors don't know," Harold said. "It's just something that happens, they told me. Sometimes someone with amnesia remembers something at first, in the early days of amnesia, and then loses it again. It could be from the swelling of the brain or whatever—I'm no doctor. Don't ask me."

But as far as I was concerned, the subject of our beds wasn't closed. I brought it up again later.

"Nobody sleeps in little beds when they're grown-up."

"Who is nobody?"

"Erma. She sleeps with her husband and they have a great big bed and it's called a king-size. And Shirley and Stan have a littler one and it's called a queen-size."

"Yes, I know all about those things. But you and I have been sleeping in twin beds for many years. You wouldn't remember, but you once thought it was a fine idea for me to sleep in my own bed. And *we* do not take our clues on how to sleep from other people."

"Well, you asked me, so I told you. You're always getting mad at me."

"I'm not mad. I'm irritated."

"I'm leaving. I don't want to talk to you anymore. You don't talk nicely to me the way you did in the hospital. You said how happy we would be when I got home and you would be nice to me and you would take me everywhere and you would buy me things."

"What things?"

"I don't now."

"Well, see? You don't even know what you're talking about. Who got you your new clothes and that new coat? It wasn't Santa Claus."

"Who's he?"

"Skip it. I've brought you stuff you haven't even put on yet. You want everything in the store. You're a spoiled child and I don't know what I'm going to do with you."

"I don't care. I don't know what I'm going to do with you, either."

"Okay, Beverly, that's enough. Now quiet down and go get a book to read."

"I don't want to read anymore. I want to go to the beach."

"This is a workday. There is no beach today. I am going out and try to earn us some money now, and I want you to be a good girl. I'll call you later. You can figure out what to cook for dinner and look up the recipe in the cookbook. Look up beef stew. Under *beef* or *stew*. That would be nice for today. Or if you see something else, take a chance."

Unfortunately, even my most recent efforts in the kitchen hadn't exactly measured up to my fantasies of delicious meals coming effortlessly out of my kitchen and winning me all sorts of praise from family and friends. Often Harold only pretended to eat or he would say he had an errand to run and would get a bite on the way. Sometimes he would still be eating a hamburger when he came in the door. No, cooking was not exactly the adventure I thought it would be.

Nor, for that matter, was housework. I began to look forward to the ringing of the telephone. That was the adventure—the unknown. Who could it be?

Sometimes when I was feeling especially lonely, it would be Shirley or Erma. They always came running if I sounded sad. Sometimes it would be Stuart, saying that he was coming over. That would make me nervous—he was still so remote and disapproving.

"You're so perfect," I said one day. "You don't do bad things like I do."

He laughed. "Perfect? Do you want me to tell you how perfect I was? I was suspended from school so many times in high school that you used to say, 'I'll never make it to forty-five. You're going to kill me before I'm forty-five.' Do you remember saying that?"

"No. Did I say that? Well, I was almost right because I died when I was forty-eight. That's three years difference." Proud that I'd figured it out, I waited for praise. Stuart just looked at me. "Well," I prodded, "wasn't I right?"

"Yes, mother, you were considered dead and they revived you. Maybe Joanie is right."

"About what?"

"She said you died and another person came back in your place. But don't feel bad. She says she likes the new person better."

But I *did* feel bad. I didn't like being two people. Who was this other one? Would I ever know her? Did Stuart think I was a different person, too?

"Everybody says you and I used to be very good friends, Stuart. Everybody says you were closer to me than you were to your father. Everybody says that."

"Yes, mother, it's true. You were the greatest. All my friends made this the meeting place. The game room was our clubhouse and you and dad left us alone and never bothered us."

"Your friends can come back. Tell them to come back."

"I know, mom, but it just isn't the same. And I'm not a kid anymore. And you don't cook like you used to, either. That was half the reason they hung around. They loved your cooking. Do you remember what you used to make?"

"Of course not. Why are you always trying to find out if I remember something? Why are you trying to trick me?"

"Don't get excited. I'll tell you what it was and maybe you'll learn to make it again. It's called *cioppino*; it's an Italian dish. All kinds of seafood go in the pot and you made a fancy red sauce for it and we'd sit around the kitchen table eating it—all the guys—and we'd sop up the juice at the bottom with Italian bread. Then we'd go back down and shoot some pool. You and dad even got me a pool table so we would have a real game room."

"I'm going to make that Italian dish. What goes in it?"

"Everything—clams, shrimp, crab meat, mussels. Oh, mom, I'd give anything to be sitting around with you and the guys, wolfing down your *cioppino* again."

Well, I did try to make it, but it was a disaster. "It's fine, mom," Stuart said, toying with a clam, "it's fine. I'm just not hungry."

But at least now I knew that my son wanted to feel closer to me. After the *cioppino*, Harold and Stuart and I stayed around the table, talking, laughing . . .

Stuart told us about his school pranks. Once he'd cut his wrist escaping through a window. Once he was expelled from the tenth grade for stealing a sheet of paper from his teacher's purse. (*His* paper, he claimed.)

"What about your friends," I asked. "Didn't they do things, too?"

"Not like I did, but they got suspended anyway, just for being near me."

"Did I go to school and talk to your principal?"

"You sure did. They would call you at work and you would come running."

"But you weren't like the kids today that I hear about." I hoped it was true, anyway. "You didn't drink or take drugs or anything really bad . . ."

He smiled.

"Oh, didn't I? I tried everything. Thank God, I got through it without getting hooked."

"Do you remember the only time I slapped you?" Harold asked.

"Do I! You knocked me halfway across the room. And all because I'd thrown one little match in the wastebasket."

"It wasn't funny," Harold said. "You could have burned the house down."

Stuart turned to me.

"See what you're missing, mother? All this nice violence. And all the cuts and broken bones. Yeah, they knew you pretty well at school."

"Well, son," Harold said, a bit sheepishly, "I never told you this, but I was in even worse trouble than you. I got hauled to the police station for mine and got a record, but you only missed a few weeks of school."

"Hey, you always said you were so perfect. So tell us what you did—it's about time."

"Well, I was just throwing a few snowballs at the people getting on the streetcars."

"That's not so bad. What's so bad about that?"

"With stones in them?"

For a long time all I could talk about was my hospital experience.

"I guess it's a miracle that I'm still alive," I told my father. "I guess I'm the only one in the family who has had a miracle like that."

"Oh, I wouldn't say that," daddy said. "Shall I tell her, Ann? Do you think she's ready for it?"

"Why not?" said my mother. "She'll see things like that don't just happen to *her.* Your father could have been a basket case but God was good to us. Well, tell her— or I'll tell her."

"Oh, tell me, tell me." I didn't have the slightest idea what they were talking about, but it sounded like quite an adventure.

"Well . . ." he began, "it was a busy day in the grocery store. Two men came in with a gun. It was in nineteen seventy-two. I was slicing meat and I looked up and a gunman was pointing a twelve-gauge shotgun at me. His partner said, 'Where's the money?' "

"What did you say?" I asked, excitedly. "Did you give it to him? Did you take the gun away from him?" I hoped it was the latter.

" 'Are you crazy?' I said, 'It's right behind you. Just don't hurt the people.' "

"Oh, all the people in the store. And then what happened?"

"They took the money and instead of getting out, one of them grabbed your mother and stuck the gun under her arm. He was aiming it at me again."

"Oh, mama, you must have been scared."

"What else? Do you think I was singing with joy? This crazy man had one arm around my neck from behind and with the other hand he's holding the gun hard against my armpit, and he's yelling, 'Where's the rest of the money, sucker?' "

I was hugging myself with fear and excitement. I could not believe such a thing had happened to this gentle-looking couple. After a moment, my father continued. "I said, 'That's all there is.' He told me again to get the rest of the money and I told him again that's all there was. He was about six feet away and he fired point-blank at me. He must have been very nervous because he missed—the bullet went through my coat and a sweater and cut the skin and flesh of my back. The doctor said another fraction of an inch would have severed my spine and I would never have walked again."

I was speechless. He had been shot. This wasn't just a fun story anymore.

"The bullet went into the wall," he continued. "I fell down and they threw your mother on top of me. Then the gunman put the gun to my head—touching my head—and he said, '*Now* where's the rest of the money?'

"Again I said, 'That's all there is,' because I was stuck with my story. If he thought I was lying maybe he would be even angrier. I held my breath, not knowing if I had said the right thing, not knowing if I was going to be dead in another second."

"Did he shoot? Did he shoot?"

"I was looking in his eyes and I didn't know what he was going to do and the other fellow—his lookout—was yelling, 'Let's go. There's too many people here.' And someone else was yelling, 'Kaufman's been shot.' All I know is that suddenly they both were running out of the store and I tried to get up from this pool of blood around me. Oh, I was so happy to be alive."

"I'm so happy you're alive, too," I said. I hugged them both, hoping with all my heart they really were my parents.

"And that was it," my father concluded. "Right after the doctor fixed me up, I locked up the place and went to Florida to rest and get my nerves back in shape, and I never did open up again. I came back in two weeks and retired, sold out."

"Oh." I was disappointed. Wasn't there more to the story? "But tell me how it turned out. How much money did they get? Did the police ever get them?"

"It's a funny thing," daddy said, "a customer had the guts to run after them. They were running down the street and they disappeared. Then he saw a meter maid and he ran to her and said, 'Did you see two men running?' and she said, 'Yeah, they went

into that house *there.'* When the police went in they were counting their money on the table, dividing it. It was one hundred
eighty dollars."

"Oh, that's a lot of money."

"Yes, but I had a couple of thousand more that they didn't get."

I felt weak. "They would have killed you if they'd found it—oh,
you took such a chance. What happened to them?"

"I don't know. I don't want to know. After the police picked them
up, they put them in the van and kept them there on the street
while they came in to talk to me. They said, 'Can you describe
them?' I said, 'I can tell you everything they wore. One had a
trench coat, one had a knitted cap, and I gave every detail."

"How come you don't tell everybody about it? If it happened to
me, I'd be telling everyone. How come, daddy?"

"My child, this is old news. It happened eight, nine years ago. I
just want to forget it. I'm telling you now to make a point. God has
been good to both of us. To you and me."

Harold was not home yet, and feeling so warm and close to
these people who most surely *must* be my parents, I started
asking them about him—was he really my husband? Had they
seen me marry him?

"Of course he is your husband. And such a good man," my
mother said. "He is like a saint the way he looks after you. You
gave him a very bad time, you know, and he has been like a saint."

"Yes, sure," added my father, nodding, "you don't know what he
has suffered. Not many men would put up with what he has
taken. You were not easy to live with."

"I know, I know," I said, "I've been a bad girl. I'm sorry. But
there's something in my mind, like he's really not my husband
and there was somebody else."

My parents looked at each other and suddenly I knew there *had*
been somebody else. "Should I tell her?" asked my father.

"Go ahead," said my mother, "she has the right to know."

In high school I had developed a mad crush on a boy and was
determined to marry him.

"It was just puppy love," my mother said. "You didn't know what
was good for you."

Apparently my parents had become alarmed because we were
too close. I was going to become a model, but my boyfriend had
changed my mind for me. He was going to become a dentist and

he wanted me to become a dental technician so that I could help out in his office.

I was stunned.

"He was too domineering," my mother said softly. "He kept you out too late. We felt he was a little wild for you. It's better the way it turned out. You have a husband who is exceptional—kind and loving and patient. We had to break it up—it was the right thing."

"But I did study and become a dental technician, you said."

"Yes, you did. You went to the University of Pennsylvania for one year and studied hygienics. And you went to work for the biggest dentist in town."

I felt funny—almost nauseated. My life had not been just a smooth fairy-princess story, after all. "Where did Harold come from? What happened to the other boy?"

"Oh, he's a very successful dentist," my mother said. "He's married and has a family, I believe. I don't think it would be good to look him up."

What was she—a mind reader? But she was right.

"What about Harold?" I asked. "Did you like him better?"

"Oh, yes," my father said. "Not that we didn't like the other boy. He was a fine young man but Harold was just right for you. And we knew his parents. Very outstanding people and they took to you right away. His mother was very gentle and refined and his father was credit manager and in charge of many people in a furniture company."

"I know them. That's Pop Pop and his wife had gray hair and wore a pink dress."

"Are you remembering?" Mama asked excitedly. "Harry, this may be the beginning."

"No, mama," I said. "Don't get your hopes up. I learned it after the accident."

She looked crestfallen.

"Oh."

Another time I begged them to tell me the story I had not wanted to hear when I first came home—the sad story of how I had been wrenched from my friends in my early teens.

"It was the only way your father could get ahead," my mother said. "He had to buy his own grocery store or he would grow old just working for other people." He had bought a small building that had a grocery store on the first floor and an apartment on the second. When he announced that I would be moving from our house to the store loft I cried every day and vowed I would not move.

"Poor child," said my mother. "You had your friends and you were very popular in school. You would have to go to a new school across town in a busy neighborhood."

"How old was I?"

"Fourteen. Just fourteen. Grandmother came to live with us, too, and she cooked a lot. I worked in the store with your father and we even had lunch in the store. We couldn't leave."

"Did I like it?"

"No, I'm sorry to say you never really got over the change. Sometimes your friends from the old school came to see you and you practically gave away the store—you loaded them up with candy and anything they wanted."

"Didn't you mind?"

My father looked incredulous.

"Mind? You were my daughter and I felt sorry for you."

"What do you mean? Why did I deserve it?"

"You would work in the store every day after school," Mama said. "Oh, you were so kind and helpful. Such a good girl. And good at school, too."

"Didn't I have any new friends at the new school?"

"Oh, yes, but it was never the same. You never stopped talking about your old school." My father sighed, then brightened. "Do you remember what you used to sleep with when you were a little girl? A Raggedy Ann doll. You wouldn't go to sleep without it. I wish you could have seen yourself."

I thought guiltily of my panda. Maybe I wasn't such a big girl after all. After some of these family sessions, Little Bev would take over.

"Oh, here comes the little girl again. You were so grown up a minute ago with all your medical dictionary words—what happened to *that* Beverly?"

"I'm not that Beverly anymore. I'm Little Beverly and I don't like you."

"Oh, my," Harold sighed, "here we go again. Come on, I'll buy you an ice cream cone."

"Oh, goody." *That* I liked. It was nice and cold on my tongue and the cone was crunchy. And afterward I was all ready for the next adventure. "Can I get a new pair of shoes? Can I have some new slacks? There's the store. Can I? Can I?"

"You have new slacks."

"They're green. I want red."

"We'll see."

"I'm going to get a job and get money and buy all the things I want and you can't stop me."

"Okay, Bev, okay. Settle down."

My mother was amazed by my hair. "You have curly hair now. I can't get over it. Why did it change? You never had curly hair."

"I know, mama. Harold told me I always wanted curly hair and now I have it."

"But what a price you paid for it," she said sadly.

"But mama, there's something else that's good, too. My high blood pressure is gone. Harold said I used to take medicine for high blood pressure and now I'm perfectly normal."

My mother looked even sadder. "Ah, normal."

"At least *that*'s normal, mama. Aren't you glad?"

"Of course, of course." She patted my arm. "And one day you *are* going to be perfectly normal and remember everything. Maybe you should go back to that corner where it happened."

"I don't want to talk about it, mother."

It was the one place I didn't want to go. I knew the address very well—Twenty-third and Chestnut streets—but it was the one place I didn't want to go.

In another attempt to spark the return of my memory, Harold had taken me there once, under the guise of our going to see if I had left any books at the Philadelphia Training School. My class welcomed me warmly but I felt foolish standing there in front of them, not recognizing one of the faces before me. Sadly, Harold led me out of the room.

"I'm sorry I put you through that, hon. I just had to try it."

My mother held out high hopes that someone at our family reunion—the occasion was my cousin's son's bar mitzvah—would make me remember the past.

But as I looked around the restaurant at all those strangers, I had never felt so alone. Even my mother with her party manners—smiling, laughing and hugging everyone—was a stranger . . .

Suddenly aware of me, she turned and took me from person to person. "Beverly, this is your Aunt Bertha and Uncle Lou . . . Here are your cousins, Carole and Maurice . . . he's Lou's son." Not knowing what else to do, I tried to shake hands with everyone. Some grabbed me and hugged or kissed me. I kissed the ones back whom I thought liked me, but I felt empty inside.

It was agony. Some people tried to remind me of something I had done in the past—"Don't you remember?" "Do you remember?" "So you don't remember?" "What do you remember, dear?"

I looked at the little bar mitzvah boy—chunky, cute in his little beanie. His *yarmulke*. It was, they told me, a word I used to know. Why did all the men wear it? Someone said it was to hide from the wrath of God. It didn't make sense. Nothing made sense. The sea of people. The cute little boy who knew me. Today he had become a man. He knew who *he* was. All these people—laughing, eating— they knew who they were. I felt sick. Lonely, lost. And there was no place to hide.

As soon as I could, I escaped to a corner of the room. I had never, ever felt so alone.

Now and then I would talk to Harold about the gray-haired lady from my hospital days. "You'd better quit talking about that," he warned me, "or someone is going to think you are crazy." I could see he hated to be reminded of the fact that his mother was dead and that he was still grieving.

"I don't care what they think. She was good to me and she looked after me."

"Please, Beverly, lay off the subject. Ghosts don't look after people. If there were such things, you could walk through them. They're like empty air. That's why they're ghosts. So if my mother came to you in the hospital, she couldn't even hand you a drink of water."

"I didn't say she did."

"And another thing," he continued angrily, "she's *my* mother, not yours. So don't you think if she was going to appear to anyone, she would appear to me, her son? Why would she appear to you? Tell me that."

"I don't know. Maybe she saw me in the tunnel going to the light."

"Oh please, Beverly, let's close this subject permanently."

So I stopped telling him . . . But the gray-haired lady returned, always when I was lying in bed, on the edge of sleep. I would tell myself that the next time she came I must ask her something, but whenever it happened, somehow I never actually spoke to her—I only listened. Most of all I wanted to ask her if I was going to live a long time. I had a feeling that there was something I had to do and after it was done, I would die.

One night the gray-haired lady told me that Pop Pop was going to get married and that I must not feel badly about it or feel sorry for her, because she understood. "He is too lonely. He cannot be alone."

Of course I didn't mention this to Harold, but I wasn't a bit surprised when Pop Pop came to us about a month later—in the autumn of 1980—and said he was going to marry a woman who lived in the same apartment house.

Hal was stunned. "I can't believe this," he said, pacing the floor. "Why did he suddenly decide to get married? It isn't even a year since mother died."

"Didn't she die just before I went into the hospital?"

"She died in December, 1979, and your accident was two months later, in February of this year."

"Anyway, I could have told you Pop Pop was going to get married. The gray-haired lady told me."

He looked at me with disgust. "Here we go again. She was your mother-in-law. Why don't you call her your mother-in-law? Why do you say 'the lady in gray' or 'the gray-haired lady,' or whatever you call her? And I still say, why would she come to you and not to me?"

"I'm sure now. I was dead and she must have seen me over there or coming through the tunnel. That's why. You never died, so she can't talk to you."

"Is that what she told you?"

"No. I just know."

"Well, next time, why don't you ask her?"

"I don't know. I don't talk to her."

"Why not?"

"I don't know."

"I see. It's just the way they do things in the spirit world. Well, may I say again, please don't get me excited about your visits from my mother. Maybe they'll just go away."

But they didn't. On her next visit she told me that another

relative had a very bad illness and would be coming to her in a few years. This time I said nothing when Hal and I later heard that this relative had gone to a doctor and learned that he would have to be placed under heavy medication.

My mother didn't think I was crazy when I told her about the gray-haired lady. "All through history, some people have had such visits, but they are very few. I remember hearing of such things once, long ago," she said.

"Harold doesn't believe it happened."

"Only you know what happened. You know, Beverly, Harold is still mourning for his mother, so if it upsets him, just don't talk about it. You don't *have* to talk about it."

"I know, but I want him to know."

"Well, sometimes people don't want to know everything. Think about whether they want to know about something before you tell them."

"I'll try. I thought everybody wanted to know everything. I want to know everything."

"Are you sure?"

"Well, I don't want to know when I'm going to die. When *anybody* is going to die. But I know she is going to tell me when it's my turn."

My mother patted my hand, too choked up to speak, and I realized that I had just told her more than she wanted to hear. But I had stopped in time—I was about to add that maybe the gray-haired lady would tell me when it was my mother's turn, too.

There was something else I did not tell my mother—that I had no fear of death for myself, but only a great fear of death for those around me. I had finally rebuilt a little world of my own, and I felt that I couldn't spare anyone in that world.

For a while, on the thirteenth of every month, Harold would remind me of the accident. I would remember the pain I felt in the hospital, the pain I felt at my first view of life, and I would think of my frustrations in trying to learn and the loneliness that was always with me. I always ended up feeling depressed.

So even after Hal stopped mentioning the monthly anniversaries, I would dread them, for they heightened my awareness of the hollowness I felt inside, the bottomless loneliness that nothing could fill. On the thirteenth of every month, I would wonder sadly what life was all about.

Sometimes I hid in my room. Why had I lived? Of course Harold would have grieved awhile, but he would have found someone else, just as Pop Pop had. Maybe someone easier to live with and more to his liking. Someone he didn't have to raise. Someone who liked sex more. Wouldn't he have been better off? And the children—they had other things to do. They didn't need me. If anything, I needed *them*. And I was an embarrassment to them. I was "My mother, the dummy."

But then one of them would phone to see how I was and I would feel guilty for my thoughts. Who was I to tell God how to do His job?

———————

"Mrs. Slater expressed a fear that her life might be going askew and at one point said, 'God has given me another life but my life might not last long. I give myself three years.' I asked her to tell me why she felt that she only had three years to live . . . and she told me that she did not know why she felt this way but she was quite certain and, for this reason, she had to get in as much as she could during that time."

10

Strictly Medical

*W*hen I had first become interested in my medical condition, I pestered Harold for details.

"You were unconscious for two or three days," he began.

"Well, which was it?" I demanded.

"Beverly, I wasn't keeping a diary. I was living hour to hour. The doctors told me your condition was grave and you weren't expected to survive, so do you think I cared how many hours it was until you opened your eyes?"

"I was just asking." Why did people always get so excited over a simple question?

"It wasn't my fault, was it?" I asked.

"No, it wasn't your fault. You can read the eyewitness account from a student at your school who saw the whole thing. I had to get it for the insurance company."

"Why did you have to get it for them?"

"Because they wanted to settle out of court." Then he started to talk about the insurance, but that still didn't interest me at all. "Tell me about the accident."

He sighed. "Well, honey, like I told you, it was a normal winter day and you were on your way to school."

"What school?" Both of us knew that I had already memorized its name.

"The Philadelphia Training School, where you taught."

"And whom did I teach?"

He sighed again. ". . . where you taught girls who wanted to become assistants to doctors and dentists. And you had already parked your car—"

"Oh, yes. I'm going to drive and teach again, right, Harold?"

"Right, little one." He patted my head. "But for now you're going to just concentrate on reading all the books I bring you that tell you about all the things you can't remember. Now, how am I going to tell this story if you keep interrupting?"

"I'll be quiet. I'll be good. And then what happened?"

"You were crossing the street at Twenty-third and Chestnut . . ."

"With the light. With the light."

". . . with the light, when a car came around the corner and hit you and flipped you onto the hood." He paused.

"And carried me—"

"Yes. It carried you about forty or fifty yards before you were thrown off and flung against the pavement, head first."

"Oh, my poor head. They fling bowling balls, don't they?"

"Well, they roll them, but you've got the idea. And then all kinds of people gathered round and somebody called an ambulance and your heart stopped in the ambulance but they saved you and it stopped again when they took you to another hospital for a brain scan to see the damage. And you were unconscious for a long time and then you woke up and we almost died of joy." Both of us laughed, thinking of how lucky I was.

"And then you woke up," he said, "and said, 'Who the hell are you' and 'I'm getting out of here.' And you know all the rest."

"You forgot something."

"What did I forget?"

I held up my hand. "The handprint."

"Oh yes, you caught me. The police found your handprint on the car's hood as if you were making a desperate attempt to ward off the car or push it away."

"And what about the blood and the black-and-blue marks?"

"Oh, my God, I don't want to think about it. You looked like something made up for Halloween—blood coming out of your ears and your hair just a clump of blood, all matted up. And they couldn't wash it for weeks. My proud beauty, why do you want me to remember you like that?"

"So you'll see how pretty I am now. I'm pretty, aren't I?"

"For a grandmother, you'll do."

"Does that mean I'm pretty?"

"Hey, to me you're better than pretty." He hugged me and I felt wonderful. What was better than pretty? I'd ask him later. Right now, I was still on the trail of my story.

"And did I have an operation?"

"No, you didn't need an operation. You had a cracked head—a line fracture in the back of the head—but they finally decided not to operate and just see what happened and whether they could control the pressure on your brain from the swelling. And they kept you pretty much packed in ice and the swelling did go down and they didn't have to open up your pumpkin head, little one. And I guess the release of the blood through the ears helped relieve any pressure on your brain, too."

"And did you ever see anyone as black and blue as me?" I asked proudly.

"Not even at the fights—not even when the guy gets thrown out of the ring." Hal was smiling. "In fact, we didn't dare show you a mirror for the longest time for fear you'd have a relapse. But I guess you would have loved the sight of every bruise."

"Of course not." I gave him a little slap. "I like me this way."

"So do I, honey. So do I. And on your own two feet. They didn't know what your physical condition would be—whether you would be able to walk again, with or without crutches. Remember, you were on life support systems for days."

"And everybody thought I would be a vegetable."

"No, everybody *wondered* but nobody was *sure* what you would be. Dr. O'Connor and Dr. LaFlare primed me not to expect too much and not to be surprised if you couldn't think and just sat around like a vegetable or turned into a violent person who would be unmanageable at home and might even have to be institutionalized. I had to think about all these things and you were pretty nutsy for a while, but now you're going to be all right, thank God."

"But you think I'm dumb."

"No, I don't. But I think you have to be patient and learn things one at a time and pay attention to papa."

"Yes, I will, Harold. I always pay attention to you." Well, a little white lie . . .

The child in me loved hearing my bedtime story, and sometimes

I even insisted Hal introduce the cast of characters in proper order . . . Prince Stuart had been the first to arrive at Graduate Hospital, where he was told that I had been taken to Presbyterian Hospital by ambulance for a brain scan. Then King Harold arrived with my royal daughter and son-in-law, Steve. Then the royal mother and father. Then Shirley and Erma. And the entourage.

Every night, before I fell asleep, I thought of my fairy tale and wondered . . . would it have a happy ending?

It was a much more sophisticated Beverly who several months later overheard Harold talking about her medical reports. From then on I pestered him to let me see them.

"This is not a storybook. This is too stark and real and detached."

"I don't care. It's about me and I want to read it."

He looked nervous.

"I don't know if it's good for you to read this stuff. I don't want you to get excited."

"I won't get excited. You think I'm a dummy. Well, I've been studying my books. I'll show you I know what things mean—medical words."

"Okay, here, take it. It's called the clinical summary. But promise if it bothers you, you'll quit reading."

I grabbed the report. "They have my name wrong. It says *Slatter.* Beverly *Slatter.*"

"Well, remember, you were an emergency patient. Correct spelling was the least of anyone's concern."

Yes, there it was, the date I already knew by heart—February 13. And I had been discharged March 30, a little more than six weeks later. The final diagnosis was that I had suffered "head trauma" and a "basilar skull fracture."

"Basilar," I said. "I know that word. It means the back of the head above the spinal column."

"It was just a crack and so they didn't operate," Harold said. "They said if there wasn't too big a buildup of blood and swelling they wouldn't have to operate and they didn't have to."

"Yes, here it is," I said. "Ugh. It says, 'She was unconscious on admission and she had significant bleeding from both nose and ears.'"

"Well, they were glad you were getting rid of the blood so they didn't have to operate."

Over and over I consulted my medical books. They had given me medication to control the swelling of the brain. Suddenly I could see myself as I must have looked to others, all black and blue and spouting tubes in all directions. Through the arm for I.V. feeding. Through the nose for oxygen. Through the mouth to ventilate the lungs. ". . . she was intubated and intravenous Mannitol was administered along with large doses of intravenous Decadron."

"Oh you were a beauty," said Hal. "And you should have seen yourself when you came back from the CAT scan. Dr. LaFlare, the resident, had gone along with you in the ambulance and he saved your life because your heart stopped and he got it started again in the ambulance."

"That was the second time I died, wasn't it." It was more a statement than a question.

"That's the way I understood it. That's what they told me. Anyway, it was something, the way Dr. LaFlare rushed in with you, barking orders at the nurses. The nurses had a laugh about it later—the way Dr. LaFlare looked. Some bottle of something had broken and here was LaFlare looking like the Statue of Liberty with his arm up, holding the tube so you'd still get the last of the precious whatever-it-was. It's funny how things are so tense and later you see the humor of it and let off steam laughing. I think it was Nurse Elaine Foos who told about it. Do you remember Nurse Elaine?"

"I don't know. I guess I would remember her if I could see her. Oh, here's something about the medication for my high blood pressure . . ."

"There's nothing like a hit on the head to make you relax."

"No. I understand. I'm not tied up inside anymore. I just say what comes to mind. That's why I don't have high blood pressure anymore. I'm glad I'm not the old Beverly. Everybody says she was quiet and all tied up inside."

"But she was a nice gal—always worrying about everyone else."

"I don't want to hear about her. I know, I'm the dummy."

"Come on now, you're growing up by leaps and bounds. Do you still want me to read that stuff or have you had enough?" He tried to take the hospital report from me.

"No, no," I protested. "I want to find out what the CAT scan said.

Oh here it is, 'The patient did receive an emergency CAT scan and this was read as enlarged right frontal and possibly left occipital cerebral contusion. The patient was brought back to the Neurologic Intensive Care Unit where she was placed on a respirator and her condition began to stabilize.' Oh, wow, listen to this. 'Her hospital course was rather stormy in the beginning in that, on her third hospital day, she developed rather severe pneumonia which the infectious disease team felt could be possibly a Staphylococcus pneumonia—' "

"Do you remember?" Harold asked. "Do you remember they had you lying on an ice sheet, a refrigerated sheet to keep your fever down and I felt so sorry for you. You were hot and you were cold and we didn't know whether to try to cover you. But they said they had to keep your poor battered head cool. Oh, poor baby, you don't remember any of that, do you? You were out cold."

"I don't know. I just know things were hazy and when I opened my eyes it was like I was seeing everything through gauze—a white haze."

"You used to pluck at the tubes as if you were trying to get them out of you, especially the one in your throat."

"Well, no wonder. It hurt. That was my first memory. The pain in my throat. It was like I was born into pain."

"But at least you were reborn and you're here. Had enough of this now?" Again he was trying to pull the report away from me.

"Wait, wait. I just want to see what it says about the amnesia." I skimmed along, not bothering to try to understand everything. "Here it is. 'Following extubation'—that means after they took the tubes out—'the patient was very slow to respond; her mentation'—I guess that's my thinking—'was rather slow and *her memory was completely gone for both current and past events.*' Hal, did you hear that?"

"Sure, I don't need them to tell me your memory was completely blank—a complete wipeout."

"I know," I said, "but isn't it eerie to have it be official? Let me go on. It says, 'She was poorly responsive to the nursing staff and barely reconized very close family members.' "

"Wrong," said Harold. "You didn't recognize any of us. I had to tell you over and over who I was and who you were and you still didn't act like you believed it."

"You're right," I said. "I *didn't* believe it. I didn't know who you were and I didn't even know if I wanted you around. Oh, Harold, would you get mad if I told you I'm still not sure you have the right person? I sometimes feel it's all a mistake and I belong somewhere else. Maybe to some other family."

"I know you do, and don't think for a minute that doesn't hurt."

But I felt no compassion for his pain. "I don't want to talk about it," I said, still scanning the report. "I'm sorry I mentioned it. Hey, ten days, I was walking around after ten days but 'still confused,' it says, and let's see, after the ten days, 'She continued to improve over the next several days and finally began to recognize her husband and her son. Speech began to return to normal in that she was able to name familiar objects and complained that she wanted to be in a regular room.' "

Harold laughed. "I might be responsible for that. I told you how much nicer it would be and you were as suggestible as a child. Once you got an idea you made a pest of yourself until everyone gave in to you—about the room, about getting home."

"I was looking for adventure. I thought getting a room was like going home. I wanted action. I didn't even know what all that was about—rooms and home. I just wanted change."

"Right. You were a little kid saying take me here, take me there."

"Well, they took me," I said defensively. "It says, 'She was subsequently transferred to Neurologic Step-Down Unit and continued to improve. On the fifteenth hospital day, she was mentally much clearer. A repeat CAT scan showed . . . contusions of both frontal and occipital areas.' Wait—let me get my medical dictionary." I ran and got the book and read aloud, " 'occipital bone—a curved, trapezoidal, compound bone that forms the lower posterior part of the skull.' That's what I thought it was. It's lucky the spinal cord wasn't severed."

"It's lucky you didn't remain a vegetable. Oh, was I happy when you finally made some sense! Joanie and I just danced around."

I looked at him. His response, his caring still didn't thrill me. Why did I have to be around him all the time? I wanted adventure.

"Where's the report?" I asked. "What did you do with it?"

"That's enough for one day, Bev. Come on, I'll take you for a ride."

Over the next few weeks I often returned to my medical records, consulting my faithful Webster whenever I came across a new word. At first I hadn't been at all interested in my Speech Pathol-

ogy record—Dr. LaFlare's initial evaluation began with the scary
and confusing line, "Receptive and expressive aphasias are evi-
denced"—but gradually I became curious to find out how I had
really sounded in the hospital.

I looked up *aphasia.* Webster described it as "loss or impairment of the power to use or understand speech." Now I was *really*
intrigued. And the rest was much easier to read, once I figured
out that *Pt.* meant patient. Me. My reception of single words was
"impaired." "Pt. is unable to identify named objects, colors or
shapes with greater than chance accuracy." I had been unable to
"select the green circle." I was able to follow simple directions but
not more complicated ones. I had "severe word finding difficulties," and I didn't seem able to produce automatic sequences, like
counting from one to ten. That came as a surprise, since I had
remembered individual numbers. The report commented on that,
referring to my "inconsistency in response pattern noted over two
sessions."

For some reason I had answered yes to all questions about
myself, regardless of whether they were in fact correct. Only once
did I say no. According to the report, "Biographical questions are
inaccurately answered."

Regarding my "cognitive status"—I looked up *cognition:* "The
process of knowing; knowledge or the capacity for it"—the report
said: "Pt. is alert, not oriented to time (dates), place, oriented to
some people." Who? I wondered. Dr. O'Connor, for sure.

From the report I learned that even at the end of the first week, I
was already making a pest of myself: "Pt. perseverates on return
home, will you help me, etc. Attention span is extremely limited,
pt. very impulsive."

The report concluded with the staff's plan to work with me and
help me increase my attention span and word power. In spite of all
my word comprehension difficulties, the report said that as far as
my own speech was concerned, I was doing quite well: "Expressive language is characterized by use of well-produced words in
sentences," though I had a tendency to omit nouns and "target"
words, which I took to mean the audience or focus of my statement.

"They keep studying the brain," Harold had once said, "but how
it works is still a great mystery. From what they tell me, medical
knowledge of the brain hasn't changed appreciably for many

years—how memory works, how memory is transmitted, how you remember how to type, for example."

"What makes you say that?" I asked. "Have you been studying?"

"No, I was just talking to Dr. O'Connor and there's lots to be learned yet. Maybe in the future your case will be better understood. Did you know your doctor wrote an article about memory years ago when he was experimenting with cats, trying to see how their memory works or can be improved or something like that? It's too complicated for me."

I went to the library and tried to find books on amnesia—without much luck.

I read the eyewitness report of the accident by a student at the Philadelphia Training School—not a student of mine, but one who recognized me anyway when she saw me walking ahead of her. Reading it was like reading about a character in a book—certainly not me. This character was walking along, carrying what looked like a bunch of books held up against her chest. She was crossing the street with the light. The car—the witness didn't know the color or make, only that it was driven by a man—was making a left turn when the car struck the character, who at once threw up her hands, as if to ward it off, and tried to back away. "The part of the car that struck Beverly Slater was right in about the dead center . . . she was actually thrown up onto the right center hood of the car . . . I remember hearing a screech sound. I cannot say if that screech sound was before the front center section of the car struck Mrs. Slater or at the time it struck her or after. All I can remember is that screech sound . . . and she was carried on the still-moving car and she was eventually dropped off that car and came to rest . . . just a couple of feet in front of the front end of where that striking car eventually came to rest.

" . . . Mrs. Slater was lying on her back. Her head was facing toward the south side of Chestnut Street . . . She came to rest on an angle. I don't know which way her feet pointed . . . When this happened a large crowd gathered. I did not run right over to where Mrs. Slater was lying on the street . . . I was just looking at her and I thought she was dead . . . "

Oh, my, it gave me a sad feeling. But for the character of the book. Not me.

11

Patchwork Quilt

I became obsessed with the mystery of me, frustrated by the conflicting stories. Who was I to believe?

Like a detective, I was scrupulously piecing together the bits and pieces of my life, fitting them into a gigantic patchwork quilt. Here, one little piece fit. There, another. I pounced on the pieces as I found them. Love, marriage, career, hopes, dreams . . .

Someone said I was married on March 11, 1951. I grabbed that little piece and wrote a note to myself to find out what year I went to college and what year I graduated from high school. My mother had said that Hal and I had married immediately after I graduated from high school—but wasn't graduation in *June?*

That piece didn't fit.

Exhausted by my constant pestering, Harold scheduled "conferences" with me so that he could have some peace and quiet."

He nicknamed me, "the bird in the Gilded Cage," and I thought it was a tribute to my love of birds. Eventually I realized it was a sarcastic reference to my decorating myself and the house in all those bright colors.

"My gilded bird," he would say. "You already have an orange rug in this house and I think that's enough color for now. Next question. No, you can't add pink sofa pillows because they look good in a friend's house. Next question, please! That subject is closed for one year."

One day Harold mentioned that Stuart loved Shirley "like a second mother." I felt a pang of jealousy. There was that word *love* again. I was sure Stuart didn't love me. Harold tried to assure me that he had been lavish with love for his mommy when he was a little boy. I couldn't believe it.

"He doesn't love me today."

"How do you know?"

"I just know."

Another little piece for the patchwork quilt was the dog—Loco had been part of the family for twenty-one years, and after he had died, a year or so before my accident, I had cried for days. "Why was he called Loco?" I asked Harold.

"Because we must have been crazy to decide to get a dog and *loco* is Spanish for crazy. And he soon lived up to his name— leaving our things strewn over neighbors' lawns, digging here and there around the neighborhood. I was afraid they would get up a petition in Mount Airy, where we used to live. You always thought they must have gotten Loco confused with some other dog and he was innocent. I swear you would have moved before you gave up that nutty dog."

"Did he like me?"

"Did he like you? He wanted to sleep with you. I had to chase him off your bed all the time. That dog sure loved you."

There it was again—*love.*

I learned that it was Fayne whom the hospital called first— strangely, her name and telephone number were the only ones found in my purse.

Now I could hardly wait for her next visit so she could tell me why I had been carrying her number around.

"I don't know, Bev," she said one afternoon. "And it bugs me. I simply can't figure it out. It's going to remain one of those mysteries of life."

I asked her to be frank and tell me what I was *really* like before the accident.

"You were nice and I liked you," she said, "but you were aloof. Do you know what I mean?"

"No."

"I mean you didn't talk to people much. You weren't friendly. You sort of had your nose in the air and even though we were friends, I didn't want to bother you. You were always so busy."

"I'm sorry," I said. "Can we be friends now?" I hugged her.

"Sure, honey, I want to be your friend. You always were my friend."

"Fayne," I said, "everybody talks about *friends*. How did you know I was your friend? How do you know a *friend*?"

"Friends do things for each other."

"Oh. What did I do for you?"

"I'll tell you what you did. Whenever my daughter Marci was having some little emergency with her braces, we would run to you. You always knew what to do because you worked for an orthodontist."

How could I have done these things I knew nothing about? With people I couldn't remember?

Fayne came to see me fairly regularly. According to Harold, she was concerned about my welfare and we shared a special bond. She was a very special friend, he said. I asked him to explain that.

Harold told me that a friend was someone you *had* to talk to if he or she talked to you. You didn't have to talk to a stranger. So I tried to sit still and listen to Fayne whenever she came over. But she seemed to be having as much trouble finding things to talk about as I did the listening.

I heard her ask Harold what he thought she should talk about. He gave a horse-laugh and said, "Try the weather."

She didn't think that was particularly funny. "Try your sexual habits," he teased. "Yours and Lennie's. Maybe that will help her adjust to a live-in husband."

She laughed lightly and said, "Fine, Harold, that's what I'll talk about, but let me do it in my own time."

I couldn't figure out this *friend* business, but I finally decided to let it rest. Instead, I asked Fayne several times to give me *her* version of the accident. She would oblige, always injecting plenty of drama into it . . .

Her phone rang early in the morning. It was a woman, saying that Beverly Slater had been very, *very* seriously injured in an accident and was at the Graduate Hospital. Did she know Beverly Slater? Fayne kept screaming, "Is she alive? Is she alive? Please tell me how bad she is," but all the woman wanted to know was whether Fayne could get in touch with the family.

Finally, the woman said, "She's very seriously injured." Fayne then made a few phone calls and rushed to Joanie's house to take care of her kids so Joanie could get to the hospital. And at the end of the day, when she got home, she realized she was still wearing her bathrobe.

Try as I might, I couldn't shake the old Bev. I felt jealous to hear Harold talk about how she loved sex, relished good food, loved the smell of pretty flowers. I tried to imagine what it would be like to be driven to finish a plate of food because of the *flavor.* What was that word people used? *Delicious.* Often Harold would look at his plate in a restaurant or a friend's house—alas, never at home—and say, "I shouldn't eat another bite of this stuff, but I just can't help it." And he would eat every bit of it.

"Well," he would say, "you can't miss what you don't know, and you'll never get fat."

"Lucky you," I would counter. "I would like just for one day to know how it feels to worry about dieting."

Odors were a different matter. Who could say I was lucky not to be able to smell flowers? Well, strangely enough, the girls could. They would tell me about having to move away from someone in a line because he or she smelled too bad. "I'll bet he hasn't had a bath in a month," they would say. Or, "I had to lean back when she talked to me."

Sometimes it seemed as though Shirley and Erma didn't really believe I'd lost my memory. Like Stuart, they kept trying to trip me up. It baffled me. Why would I want to *pretend* not to remember?

Didn't they know how I longed to fathom the past? How I longed to be a part of the world that remembered?

They talked about their children. One of them had given birth to babies easily. One had been in labor longer. They had to explain about labor.

"It isn't fair," I said. "I gave birth to grown people. I even gave birth to a grown girl with two babies of her own . . . Do you know how terrible that is? I want babies."

As I matured, I would wake up at night yearning to know what it felt like to give birth to a baby. And what it was like to be getting married. And to go to school and have friends my own age.

Erma and Shirley assured me we had been friends almost all our lives. We were the three musketeers. The inseparables. Since I couldn't seem to shake them—no matter how dull and boring and childish I acted—I finally accepted and even learned to enjoy them. Most important, they were the key to my past. I could ask them things I didn't want to ask Harold or my children. I could talk to them about anything. They didn't laugh.

"Do you like sex?" I asked one day, out of the blue.

"Sure, you bet," they answered, almost in unison.

"Well, I don't," I said. "I hate it."

"You used to like it."

"How do you know?"

"You used to talk about it. We all did. You'd better not mention this to Harold," they said. "Men don't like to think you're talking about them as lovers."

"Why?"

"They might think you're comparing them to some other man who's a better lover. Every man wants to be the greatest lover."

Oh, my, it certainly was educational around these girls. But I still wasn't going to pretend I liked sex if I didn't. The panda would help me get out of it. The panda was the one thing I didn't tell even my understanding friends about. Somehow I felt this might turn them against me. I had carefully examined their homes and *they* had no pandas or other stuffed animals lying around.

I started to become more and more curious about my two tour guides to the past. Before they had simply been kind ladies who did things for me and took me places and kept me company. Now they were emerging as individuals.

I called them whenever I had a problem—even a trivial one, like where do you put the cup and saucer when serving company— and they always answered without laughing or telling me that they were too busy or that I was interrupting. And often they would call to check up on me. "Have you used the air freshener? Have you put on perfume?"

But they couldn't teach me to eat red meat. They would order it for me and I would just let it sit. I was satisfied with my salad.

This wasn't anything new; even before the accident I hadn't eaten much red meat—if any—for years. How did the body know what it used to like even while it couldn't taste or know the difference?

"There must be some kind of memory in the body concerning certain strong likes and dislikes and fears that is retained even when the memory of people and events is gone," said Shirley. I agreed. Fear of heights, fear of being closed in, dislike of raw onions and red meat . . . it couldn't be just a coincidence.

The mustard was another surprise. One day, while Harold and I were shopping, I picked up a bottle of dark mustard. He said, "I like yellow mustard," and then became quite excited. "I'll be damned. I guess you don't know, babe, that you always got two bottles of mustard—dark for you and yellow for me—and here you are still choosing dark. I've got to talk to the doctor about this."

I was about to toss the dark mustard into the shopping cart but Harold stopped me. "You don't need that mustard. Why should we pay for two bottles of mustard when you can't taste mustard anyway?"

"I know, Harold," I said, "but I just can't help it. It's something inside me." He walked down the aisle toward the catsup and I tossed the mustard back into the cart, hiding it under the paper towels to be sure it got safely home.

There were so many little mysteries to ponder . . .

Stuart still tried to jog my memory. "Do you remember when I dated that Italian girl?"

"No," I said. "Did you? What happened?"

"We broke up," he said. "Before I went to college."

"Oh. I'm sorry."

"No, it's okay. I'm dating another girl now."

"Is she Italian?"

"No, she's Spanish. I'm going to bring her home to meet you. You'll love her. She's very kind. She wants to meet you. Her name is Mari Costra, pronounced like 'Mary' with an 'ah.' Her father is a teacher like you. He teaches Spanish to Americans going overseas."

"Oh, does she work, too?" I was very conscious of people's jobs. I couldn't get over how many occupations there were—and how they all meshed together so that people could help each other. Hal helped people have better houses. The sales clerk helped you pick out a pair of slacks. Doctors helped people get well.

"Yes, she does work, mother. She has a good job. She is working for a brokerage firm in New York. She still lives with her family. They are very old-world and protect her very carefully."

"Oh?" I said, "How can you see her if she's there and you're in Philadelphia?"

"I go up every other weekend and stay with her parents. They're very good to me. Her mother speaks mostly Spanish and not too much English. I'm learning some Spanish now to talk to her."

"Oh."

"I want her to come visit me and spend the weekend here with you—she's not permitted to visit me at my apartment."

"Oh, wonderful. I would love the company. I'll fix the seafood dish you like."

"No, mother. Promise you won't. Just fix chicken and whatever else you fix for dad."

When I met her, I liked her very much. She was small and gentle and kind. I was so glad I was not intimidated as I sometimes was when I met a woman who immediately demanded to know all about how it felt to have amnesia.

Mari so carefully avoided asking me anything that soon I found myself telling her all about it.

I was sorry to see her leave. It must be nice to have a daughter living at home, I thought. I wondered what it was like when Joanie was growing up . . . Now that Joanie and I were so close, it was hard to believe that Stuart had once been my favorite.

"But mother, you're a different person," she said. "I like this person much better. This person isn't stiff-nosed and always on my neck." She hugged me. "Always be this person, even if you get your memory back," she said.

"I think you're safe," I said. "The doctors aren't very hopeful about anything changing. But tell me, how could you tell I was partial to Stuart?"

She laughed. "You gave him everything he wanted. I had to fight for everything. I'll give you the perfect example. Do you know that you and daddy gave Stuart a college graduation present of a trip to Europe when he graduated Rutgers?"

I was amazed.

"I did? We did?"

"Yes, you did. *You* were the one who insisted he deserved it. Five weeks in Europe—the lucky dog. He and his friend, you know, Steve Kominsky, went together and backpacked in a bunch of countries."

"I'm sorry. I'll try to make it up to you, Joanie."

She hugged me again. "Don't worry about it, mom. Just be the pal you are now."

One day, Joanie announced that she was thinking of going back to college to take some art courses. "Why art?" I asked.

She looked hurt. "Aren't you aware that those are my paintings?" She pointed at the walls. "I studied art in college."

"I'm sorry."

"No, you're fine. You're getting there. You're starting to put things together, mom. I'm so proud of you."

She was proud of me! *Me.* Whoever Beverly Slater was, I was beginning to like her.

———————————

"But she would frequently cry and seemed extremely unhappy at times. It is interesting to note how rapidly her mood would change and that she could be happy and laughing moments after she had obviously been quite sad. She referred many times to the fact that it was the thirteenth of the month and seemed to be worried about what might happen."

12

The Heart of an Onion

I was like an onion. As I peeled away each layer, something new was revealed and there was always another layer beneath. I was convinced that at the heart of the onion was the real Beverly. But how many layers would it be before I found her?

I knew Joanie would tell me the truth. "There's one thing I'd like explained," I said. "I know I was terrible in the hospital, but in what way? Please tell me what I was really like. Was I really so bad?"

"Well, at first you were full of tubes, of course, with your eyes closed. Tubes, tubes, down your throat and in your nostrils and you couldn't even speak when your eyes did open. But after the tubes came out and after you *could* speak, you were like an animal, a snarling jungle cat. You'd lash out with your hands. And of course you cursed and said every vile thing. I can't tell you how frightening it was, how awful.

"I remember once I went out in the hall with daddy and we both cried. I couldn't imagine this was going to be my mother for the rest of my life, but daddy said that we had to be ready for anything because even the doctors didn't know what was going to happen. What you would be. Maybe we would have to put you in a home if you were going to be violent all your life. And I wondered if you would want to live if you could see yourself."

"Sometimes," I said, "I wondered, too, if I wouldn't have been better off dying. Sometimes I still do."

"Oh, mom, don't think that way. You've come so far. You've come such a long way."

"If I've come so far, why do I feel such a mystery to myself? Who am I?"

For a long moment we sat smiling at each other. "Mother," Joanie said, "do you know that when you had the accident, you had all these valentines in your purse with our names?"

"I did that?"

"Do you know how important Valentine's Day was to you? I don't know why. Maybe it's because you didn't use to like to show affection but you could say it in a card. Anyway, would you believe, the worst I ever made you feel was when I didn't buy you a valentine?" I hugged her. "You don't have to send me valentines anymore. You're so pretty, you look like a valentine. I feel so good when people say we look alike."

"Forget it, mother. Whether you like it or not, you're getting your valentines. I can't go through that trauma again."

I pulled out some half-finished needlework that I had found on a shelf and she showed me how to make the stitches. I worked at it for a while, but eventually reported back to Joanie that it was just too boring. "I'd rather read a book or talk to people. I don't like to sit alone in the house sewing. I want to be out with people."

From Joanie I learned what the early years of my marriage had been like. "I was a storefront baby," she would say. "You put me in a playpen down in the store and all the grocery customers would watch over me and play with me. They would look in the front glass and wave at me and I would wave back. I thought I belonged to everybody. Everybody was an auntie or an uncle."

"Why were you down there?"

"Because you went to work and grandma was supposedly taking care of me. You know, we lived above the store till I was three or four or so."

"And I worked?"

"Yes, as far back as I can remember, you always worked. I think you wanted to help buy a house. That was the dream you were always talking about, and finally you did buy this house and you were so happy about it—and about those pillars out front."

I felt very grown-up talking to my grown-up daughter this way

. . . but then my mood would change and I would be on the floor, playing with my panda or trading costume jewelry with Aryn—as long as Hal was safely out of the house. "I want the red beads." "No, they're mine." "You can't take them." "You can have the blue ones—they're bigger." "No, give me back my red beads." "I'll trade you for these chains." "Okay."

And so it went. Sometimes we played house. I was the mother and Aryn the father. Perri was the baby and we would scold her for everything we could think of. Harold would come in, take one look at me sounding like a four-year-old, and shake his head, saying, "Now I'm raising a third child."

Now and then, whenever I was being an adult, Joanie would play amateur psychologist . . . "I think I know why you resented me but accepted Stuart. It's because you got pregnant with me almost right away and spent what should have been still the honeymoon period vomiting and feeling terrible. And your first wedding anniversary found you in the hospital giving birth to me—you never could be a lighthearted bride."

"And Stuart came four years later," I added.

"Yes. And by that time you were perfectly adjusted to life, marriage, and motherhood. So you didn't resent him and you could have fun with him. Oh, how I used to wish you'd have fun with me the way you had fun with him."

"Did you hate me?"

"No. I just knocked myself out trying to impress you. But at least daddy was impressed, so I avoided growing up into a neurotic child—or at least no more than normally neurotic."

Then Joanie remembered the time I had been on an honesty kick, and she had come home with what she claimed was an *A* on a test. When I looked at the paper, it read *A-* and I was furious—not because *A-* wasn't a fine grade, but because she had lied to me. I told her that I would not have a liar in my house and ordered her outside, locking the door.

Poor Joanie had stood outside blubbering until I felt she had learned her lesson.

As I listened, I felt like crying. "Oh, Joanie, I'm so sorry. How could I have done that to you? I love you."

"Oh, Mother, you don't know what it means to me to hear you tell me you love me. I know you used to love me but you never told me. But maybe something good came of it, because I give my kids all the love and kisses they can hold.

There was no end, or so it seemed, to things I didn't know . . .

All of Stuart's friends used to have kitchen privileges. I would stock our refrigerator with the finest sandwich meats, and they would keep careful track of our corned beef and pastrami supplies. Once Harold had said, "Would you guys mind holding it down to one sandwich apiece? I'm going to have to take out a second mortgage."

Like Stuart, Steve raved on and on about my *cioppino.*

I was surprised to learn that Stuart had bought a car.

"How could he afford it when he was in high school?" I asked.

"Oh, didn't you know?" said Steve. "We worked all through high school. We did all kinds of things, but our best job was as salesmen in a sporting goods store. It was a riot. You know," he said, "you used to be like a second mother to me, but I sure like the new you. You're a regular guy. I could never have talked to you like this in the old days. You wouldn't have laughed. You would have looked very stern and shocked. Did you know your son is afraid of heights?"

"He is?" I was shocked. "I'm afraid of heights, too, and I hate elevators. I'm afraid to go up alone."

"Well, he's not that bad," said Steve, "but when I went up in the Eiffel Tower in Paris and was going to take pictures from the observation platform, he wouldn't go and he gave me his camera to duplicate whatever I did with my camera. He didn't want anyone to know he couldn't stand being out in the open at a great height."

Could fear of heights be inherited? I decided to ask Dr. O'Connor the next time I saw him.

One day Erma arrived with a little pile of poems that I had written during various sessions with the group. "I was afraid to show these to you before," she said. "I didn't want you to be sad. But first take a look at something else I found. Read this carefully and you'll see something astounding."

It was Joanie's engagement party invitation. The date leapt off the page . . . *February 13, 1972.*

"I'm not showing it to you to make you sad," Erma said. "I'm trying to show you, don't you see, that good things have also happened on February thirteenth. See? Joanie and Steve went on to get married, and nothing happened."

"I can't help it," I said, "I wish I didn't know it. It puts a cloud on it. I'd like to cross it off the calendar."

She laughed.

"Not a bad idea. Do you know, many buildings have no thirteenth floor because nobody wants to rent there?"

"I can believe it. I want to crawl into a hole and hide every thirteenth."

Quickly she changed the subject. "The group said we had our own poet-in-residence. I read some of the invitations and chuckled. I may have been serious and aloof, but I did have a light touch.

The group's invitation to Erma and Bob's twentieth wedding anniversary read:

> We think it is time for your four peers
> To cook up a dinner for you two dears
> The twenty-ninth of Sept. is your *china* day
> But we're choosing the twenty-fourth, if we may.
> The hour is eight so don't dare delay
> Or you'll sit in a corner and may not play.
> 34 South is natch the place
> The Wolfs and Slaters will tickle your taste.

In 1977 I had really gone all out for Shirley and Stan's twenty-fifth wedding anniversary, on January fifteenth.

A few friends and relatives had pooled their resources and were sending them to Hawaii. Harold and Bob, Erma's husband, had each chipped in $500. I couldn't believe we had once been able to afford such gestures. Now Harold wouldn't let me buy anything.

Had he changed? Was he generous with other people and not with me?

I started to feel angry, but soon I was engrossed in reading the poem I'd written for Shirley and Stan:

SHIRLEY AND STAN
(Celebrating 25 big ones)

The twenty-fourth year brought sickness and trouble
The twenty-fifth year begins with a bubble.
Our happy group said, What to do? What to do?
We're so grateful to still have the two of you.

Since the most important recipe in life
Is health, happiness and very little strife,
We decided to give you our own recipe.
Listen to the doctor—follow carefully:

Take three days at Waikiki
Sit on the beach, enjoy, sightsee.
A pinch of Pearl Harbor is a must
And Diamond Head is for extra thrust.
Add five days on Mauna Kea
Dance on a terrace. Golf from a tee-ah.
A drop of swimming and tennis, too,
Oh! How we wish we could all join you.
Bake for eight days with all our love
And come back with snapshots of two turtledoves.

We chose the date after much debate.
We couldn't leave weather to fickle fate.
January, February it rains, you know,
So March ninth is the time to go.
Shirley won't have to miss night school—
It's the Easter break. We're no fool.
And for Stan a much deserved store rest
After the Xmas and Valentine mess.

Shirley and Stan, please understand,
There's nothing up our sleeves, nothing underhand.
This is one time you can have it all your way.
You may add a day or decide not to stay
Whatever you wish to do, do do—
The money may be refunded, too.

Erma said the last line brought down the house. "England had
its poet laureate but our group had *you.*" I laughed. "You know,

Erma," I said, "I'm still interested in poetry and I've been memorizing some. Isn't it strange?"

"So your personality hasn't changed that much after all, has
it?"

Suddenly I had an inspiration—maybe the reason I had had
Fayne's number in my purse was that I was going to suggest we go
into the greeting card business to do verse invitations. It wasn't
so farfetched—Fayne was involved in her husband's printing
business, and I knew that I'd already been involved in a money-
making scheme with Evelyn Portnoy for our Tooth Fairy Game.

I almost laughed aloud. Here I was, peeling away the layers of
the onion, and beneath the frustrated cook, the would-be teacher,
the confused mother, the bumbling wife, and the stumbling
friend, beat the heart of something quite unexpected—a fledgling
poet.

V

HITTING BOTTOM

13

SLIPPING,
SLIDING

*I*t started simply enough.

Harold announced that he had given up the Atlantic City beach apartment. "But why?" I wailed. "I like it."

"Too much outgo and not enough income. I can't handle a mortgage payment *and* the apartment rent. Do you know what our expenses are?"

I didn't want to hear. "But what will I do? I like the water. I like the sand."

"We can still go. We'll rent a room for a weekend now and then. I promise."

He was chopping up my little world and I didn't like it one bit. "You won't keep your promise." I stalked off. He followed me, held me in his arms, and assured me he would.

He did take me now and then, that summer of 1981, but he wasn't much fun, always grumbling about the cost of things. I tried not to pay any attention. Money just wasn't a part of my world. Joanie and Stuart were, Shirley and Erma were, Evelyn Portnoy was, Harold, of course was, my search for a new job was . . . but not money.

Since March I had been a lady of leisure and leisure just wasn't my bag. It *had* given me time to explore my past with Shirley,

Erma, and Evelyn, but I was feeling that old desperation for a way to prove myself.

Although I could drive, I still wanted Harold to take me on job interviews. He didn't go into the room with me, but I somehow felt safer if he came along.

Complaining that I was taking time from his business, he would cancel his own appointments to accompany me. Even when he was just sitting around the house brooding, he still seemed reluctant to take me. No, there wasn't much fun in that summer of 1981 . . . except for when I buried myself in my books.

"Do you know what *lysis* means?"

"No. I'm going broke and you're bothering me with trivia."

"It's not trivia. It's very important. It means destruction."

"Oho, just the right word for me."

"And do you know what *my* means?"

"Of course. You're talking about *my* destruction."

I laughed, oblivious to his meaning. "It means muscle. So whenever you see *myolysis*, it means destruction of the muscle. And if it's the nerve that's destroyed, that's *neurolysis*, do you get it?"

"I get it, all right. My nerve is being destroyed every day. You try going out there and finding the customers and then trying to please them. Do you know someone is suing?"

"Oh, really, why?" But I was only mildly interested.

"Because he claims the job was incomplete and . . ." I tuned out the rest. I tuned back in as he commented that he would have no objection to my taking a more ordinary job. "You apply for only the hard jobs that you can't get. Medical things. Why don't you answer the ads for the simple jobs? I could use your help."

I ignored him. I had no interest in the household finances and couldn't have cared less that Hal had taken my checks from my consumer job and had put them in his account.

"I'll find a job in medicine, Hal. You'll see."

"Sure, sure. When hell freezes over."

I read every ad in the want-ad section. One day there was an ad for a medical secretary-teacher and I sent in the old Beverly's résumé. A few weeks later, I was called for an interview. I was thrilled. At least my Other Image was good for something.

The interviewer seemed glad to have found me.

"I see that you were a supervisor and teacher in a school that trained medical assistants. That is exactly what we are looking for—someone with experience. Why did you leave that job?"

I suddenly realized she didn't know about my amnesia, and my heart sank. "For health reasons," I said. "I had to leave for health reasons, but that's all right now."

"Good," she said. "You may be just the person we need." She explained that I would be teaching underprivileged young women to become medical secretaries and office assistants. The checks would come from Camden Community College, but the course was funded by CETA—Comprehensive Employment Training Agency. CETA leased part of the facilities of the college. The program was called VIP Secretarial. Apparently a replacement was needed immediately.

"I can start today," I said, laughing.

"Well, it's not quite that urgent. Oh, I should mention that along with handling a doctor's office, keeping records, and checking a few simple things—blood pressure, pulse, temperature—you'll have to handle billing and medical math problems."

I must have looked alarmed because she hurriedly added, "Of course, you will have the teacher's textbook and the key book with all the answers."

I brightened. Of course. And anything I didn't know about math, I could check with Harold.

The director showed me around the school, explaining my duties more fully. With my experience, she said, I would have no trouble explaining how to take blood pressure, pulse, and temperature. Having recently read up on it and practiced on Harold, I was sure *I* knew what I was doing. But would I be able to explain it? Still, this wasn't the time to show my insecurities. "No problem," I said.

I wouldn't have to bother with EKGs, she said, but I *would* have to show students how to make out insurance forms, especially Blue Cross-Blue Shield.

I kept telling myself that certainly I could follow instructions. Or could I? Oh, my, she still wasn't finished with her list . . .

I would have to give a basic typing course so the students could type up medical forms and their employer's medical notes. That was a foul ball. Had I ever typed? I'd have to ask Joanie—she typed all the time.

"I'm not really a typing teacher—" I began.

"Oh, don't worry," she said. "If you come to work here, you'll have a typing book that blocks out every lesson. A lot of time in class is spent just in practicing for speed."

"Oh," I said, trying to sound casual. This was getting scarier all the time. Here they were talking about speed, and I didn't even know how to type my first word!

I rushed home and asked Hal if I had ever typed.

"I don't think so," he said. "In fact, I'm pretty sure you never typed. You never mentioned it."

I called Joanie. "Of course you typed. Not very well, but I think you learned when you worked for the dentist. Why are you asking?"

"Because I'm coming over right now, if you're not too busy, for an emergency refresher course. I may have to teach it."

"Heaven help us."

"It's only a little part of what I may teach. The main thing is how to be a medical secretary."

"Wow! Well, come on over. The kids are in bed."

She showed me where to put my fingers on the keyboard, how to space, punctuate, use numbers and symbols—especially the dollar sign. "If they work for a doctor they'll probably wear out that key." We both laughed. She asked what I would be earning and I told her "Over two hundred fifty dollars. Really? Beats unemployment!"

"And benefits," I added. "Retirement benefits, insurance. But I have one more question—what's a speed typing test?"

"Mom," she said, shaking her head , "you sure have guts. You're sure not the mother I used to know."

"The timid one is dead," I said. "Forget her."

"Never. But I love you, too." And she hugged me. Here we go with the love again, I thought. But I was learning what it meant.

To Harold's amazement, I got the job. "I'm sorry for my lack of faith," he said, "but they didn't see you in the hospital the way I did or listen to all the questions you asked, so they don't have doubts about what you know and what you don't know."

"That doesn't matter anymore. I know I can handle anything. I can look it up. I'm going to have a key book with all the answers."

"Well, anyway," he said, "they're doing a good deed in taking you and you're doing a good deed in helping all those deserving kids from poor backgrounds go out and get good jobs for themselves. I *know* you're going to knock yourself out for them."

Did I detect a note of sarcasm in that last statement?

"What are you trying to say?" I asked sharply.

"Just don't overdo it. Don't try to be a mother to everybody. This is not the consumers' office. I don't want you to wear yourself out."

"Don't worry. I'll just do what I'm supposed to do. That's all."

The first day of school, I was completely on my own. I looked at the students and they looked back at me. I looked into my desk and found what looked like the key with all the answers, but the first question showed me that not all the answers were included. I pulled out my medical dictionary.

Before I knew it, the first class was over—I hadn't realized that classes changed every forty minutes. In my first forty minutes of teaching, I had given a test and answered several technical questions. And now I had papers to take home and grade. I felt like a real pro!

There were two other teachers handling the medical secretary classes, but we were all kept so busy that we rarely got to see each other. Other teachers handled computer secretaries and executive secretaries.

Of course, Hal was right. As soon as I had gotten over my initial panic at facing a class with a wiped-out memory, I loved each and every one of my students and felt a personal concern about whether they would measure up and get jobs. The girls came to me with every kind of question—even questions about their personal lives—and I answered them as best I could. If I didn't know what to say, I'd tell them to talk to me about it tomorrow, and went home to discuss it with Harold or one of my girl friends.

I was always a chapter ahead of the class. The course was set up so that the girls studied the chapter and took a test before proceeding to the next chapter. Correcting the tests was easy because they were standardized and already printed and the answers were in my key book.

So, things were looking up. I had a job. *I was needed.*

One day late in September of 1981, Hal came home very upset. He didn't want to talk about it, but he did say that his partner had called to tell him that the business was in deep trouble and he needed to come over right away. They talked in the family room-office. After his partner had left, Hal came in and said, "We're going bankrupt. Butch has decided to file for bankruptcy."

"What does that mean to us?" I had learned what bankruptcy was . . . but only as something that happened to other people. Not us.

"It means I've got to find another job. It means I don't know if I'm going to get my commissions on the last jobs I sold."

I had a terrible thought. "Does this mean all my insurance money is gone?"

"I'm afraid so. Butch says he'll try to salvage something for me, but it doesn't look good. He doesn't even have money for the lawyer we need. I have to go with him tomorrow to see the lawyer and I have to bring the money to pay him."

Money for the lawyer didn't seem too important to me, but what made me really resentful was the fact that all my money was gone and Hal hadn't even said he was sorry. He hadn't even bought me anything special for my money! I'd been the one who suffered and I'd been tricked out of my reward!

I didn't know what to say and I was afraid to show my anger. I picked up one of my medical books and began reading. After all, I reasoned, I *had* said he could take the money. I decided to put the whole matter out of my mind. Somehow Hal would manage.

"Why don't we go shopping?" I suggested. "I want to buy some new clothes for my new job. The other teachers have new outfits all the time."

"Beverly," he said angrily. "Aren't you listening? I'm telling you we're in financial trouble. You're not buying anything."

I started crying.

"It's my money!"

He wasn't moved.

"This is a family and it's our money. *I'm* the head of the household and *I* decide what to do with it. I don't like to be tough but these are tough times. I've been humoring you long enough—the party's over."

"I've been humoring *you*. You don't let me have anything."

"You're a spoiled child."

"I am not. You're bossy and I hate you."

"That's about the thanks I expected for just about wrecking my life, my career, and my mental health getting you to this stage."

"*You* didn't get me here. You didn't even think I could get a job."

"All right, rub it in. You're doing better than I am right now."

He looked so depressed. "All right," I said, "you can have my money. You always take it anyhow."

He looked *really* angry.

"I don't want it. I'll make out somehow. I have a possible client I'm working on."

That certainly took the wind out of my sails. I had felt pretty important when Hal said he needed my money. Now he was spurning it—and me. We fought some more. Suddenly I had a sobering thought. What would I do if Hal got really angry and refused to help me with my math problems?

Back in the classroom, typing was my biggest problem. I decided that honesty was the best policy . . . I told the students that I couldn't type, but that we would figure it out together. I would read aloud from the manual to answer their questions, and while they were typing I would practice myself. I was sure I was the worst in the class and I didn't mind admitting it . . .

"Just because I sit behind a big desk doesn't mean I know more than you do." Unfortunately this got back to management and was not well received.

"I have to be honest," I said to the supervisor. "I'm learning a lot from the students and they're learning from me."

That wasn't the end of my honest approach. "The reason I sit behind this desk," I said another day, "is not because I have a higher IQ or am smarter than you, but because I help you find the right answers. If I don't know the answer right away, I'll find out where we can get it and bring it to you the next day."

They never asked where I got my answers, so I kept my battalion of teaching assistants (Erma, Shirley, Joanie, and Hal) a secret. And in spite of their blunt teacher—or perhaps, I like to think, *because* of her—a lot of those girls really learned something!

A few students said they liked me because I didn't put on airs. Others appreciated the fact that I would take my lunch hour to help them with problems.

I learned along with everyone else—or rather, one day before everyone else—how to divide words between syllables, how to contract two words into one, how to write sums of money, where to allow breaks at the end of the line in writing dates or addresses.

It was a whole new world. I had not realized how careful one had to be in writing a business letter—but then, I didn't write business letters at home. Harold took care of everything—bills, correspondence, banking. When I realized I knew nothing of how much money we had in the bank, I asked him about it, and he said that he didn't know off hand but that one day we would go over the whole thing. That day never arrived.

Eventually I forgot about it. Harold gave me money for lunches and outings with Joanie or my friends, but I spent most of my free time learning—it made every day so exciting! I think I was more thrilled than my students when we studied the section of the typing manual headed "Frequently Confused Words": *all ready* and *already; precede* and *proceed; respectively* and *respectfully; forth* and *fourth; their* and *there,* and on and on . . .

One thing I finally got clear in my mind was that though we were located at Camden Community College, we were actually a separate entity. I was not teaching in a college but in a government-sponsored program that happened to be located at a college. I kept studying my old books, hoping that someday I would teach again in a school that had its own facility, not borrowed space.

Harold seemed more sympathetic about my constant studying, and when I told him that I needed a book to help me study all the words in my medical dictionary, he went with me in search of such a book. Soon I was the proud possessor of *Medical Terminology,* by Genevieve Love Smith and Phyllis E. Davis.

Poring over my new bible, I tried to tune out Harold's rantings about his partnership. The lawyer handling the bankruptcy case said he needed more money, and again Butch, saying he was broke, asked Harold to take care of it. This time Harold told Butch and the lawyer, "I did not sign any papers. I'm not truly a *real* partner. I invested money in this business on only a handshake. *This* is the end of the line. And I'm signifying the end of the so-called partnership with the wave of *this* hand. Good-bye, gentlemen."

He had walked out of the lawyer's office, leaving the two men standing there, speechless. "Now we're both like you, Beverly," Hal said. "We're both starting over."

For a few weeks, Hal tried selling phones or phone services. I wasn't clear on it and hardly paid attention. Then suddenly he was back in the business he liked, home improvements. But this time he was an independent again, getting jobs and turning the contracts over to various companies to do the work.

Suddenly it looked as though my husband didn't need me, at least not as much as my friend Shirley—her whole life seemed to have fallen apart.

In the second summer of my new life I had noticed that Shirley and Stan weren't sitting close together on the couch anymore. She seemed to be trying to move closer to him, to touch him, but he kept moving away. It puzzled me. This wasn't like the Stan I knew . . . Didn't he see the love in Shirley's eyes?

As the fall of 1981 approached, Shirley confided to Erma and me that Stan had refused to go on vacation to Israel with her, the trip they had dreamed of for years.

"What are you going to do?" we asked.

"I'm going alone," she said. "Well, not exactly. I've lined up two unattached women who want to go along. I'm going to enjoy this trip. I've waited too long."

She went. When she got back, she called me, sobbing. "Stan has left me. He wants to be alone and find himself."

I rushed over to her house. Erma was already there. Shirley was inconsolable. "I can't bear to see his clothes," Shirley said. "He's coming to pick them up."

"He'll bring them back," I said. "He'll come back. How will he know what to eat if you don't tell him?" It was definitely the wrong thing to say. She wept bitter tears again.

Later Harold gave me *his* theory of what had happened. "Stan found out he could survive nicely all by himself and he rediscovered good food and the joys of making up his own mind about things."

Stan moved in with a male friend until he could find an apartment. Harold visited him and came home with a report.

"I think what happened to Stan is that he came close to dying, just like you did, and now he wants to live, really live, and do everything he missed. He's eating everything he shouldn't and loving it. I don't know—he seems very happy. He says he doesn't care how long he lives, he's going to enjoy life."

I thought of Shirley and all her concern for Stan's every move because of his health . . . and I realized that nobody could live someone else's life for him.

What a puzzle life was! And sometimes not too pleasant a one.
The phone rang. "Hello?"

"Your car," an irritated voice said. "Your car is overdue."

"But what's *overdue?* Is it due there for a tune-up?"

"Look, you're his wife, aren't you? Aren't you the wife of Harold
Slater?"

"That's what they tell me."

"Look, this isn't funny. We're considering repossessing."

"What's repossessing?" A new word.

"That does it. Look, just tell your husband if he doesn't get his
payment in immediately, we'll have to take the car back."

Harold was always saying, "Get it down on a piece of paper," but
today I didn't *have* a piece of paper and now I couldn't remember
what the nasty voice had said. Was he going to make me feel like a
dummy again?

"Oh, Harold," I said, "a man called and got angry about the
car—do you know what made him angry? He said some word
about possessing."

"What number did he leave?"

"I didn't get his number—"

"What have I been telling you about taking numbers? How
many times have I told you about numbers?"

"Oh, here we go—here's the dummy again."

"You said it, not me. But that was a pretty smart observation."

"I'm leaving."

"You're leaving?"

"Yes, and I'm never coming back." I walked to the door. Now was
the time for him to come running after me and take me in his
arms and tell me not to go.

"Good-bye."

I couldn't believe my ears. "I'm never coming back."

"I said good-bye. Take care of yourself."

Standing in the doorway, I suddenly understood. I didn't really
want to go. I just wanted to be hugged and forgiven.

I ran back into his arms. He didn't say anything. I didn't say
anything. So much for running away.

But there was still the problem of the bills. The phone calls
about overdue payments persisted. Harold didn't explain anything—he just said, "I'll take care of it," and then he'd cuss a little
under his breath.

"Mr. Slater did not appear to understand his wife's difficulty in dealing with situations and, on the surface, presented himself as being quite intolerant of her inability to comprehend his problems. However, on probing, it became evident that he was really quite bewildered, upset, and embarrassed at his own inability to cope."

14

A Fireplace
Scene

*I*t was a cold December, 1981.

One night when I came home, I snapped on the light switch and nothing happened. I turned the knobs on the stove and nothing happened. The house was freezing cold. I paced the floor, waiting for Harold. It was too dark to read. I felt my way to the bathroom. At least the toilet still flushed. And the water still ran from the faucets, although there was no hot water.

When Harold finally arrived, he found me curled up in a living room chair, crying. "What's wrong with this house?" I blubbered. "Nothing works anymore."

"Oh, rats," he said, "I forgot to pay the gas-light bill."

Now it was *my* turn to be angry.

"How could *you* forget? I'm the one who forgets, not you."

"Well, you're going to have to learn the facts of life. I'm human and I'm slowly going to pieces and I haven't paid the bills because I've been too busy with you."

"Oh, it's my fault," I wailed as he fumbled with a candle. "I'm the dummy but I'm not that dumb. It doesn't take that long to pay a bill. You write a check and you mail it."

"Yes, you do—if you have money in the bank. I'm broke, Beverly. This is the end of the line. I owe people. The business is broke. I'm broke. But listen . . . somehow I'll get the money. I've taken care of you so far, haven't I?"

"I don't know." I was furious. My husband takes my insurance money, spends all of it, and calls *that* "taking care of me"? "I'm mad," I said. "I don't like this. It's not fair."

"Well, hold your fire. Life isn't fair. I'm going outside for wood." Life isn't fair—don't expect it to be fair. That's what Shirley and Erma always said.

Soon he had a fire blazing in the fireplace. I sat on the rug, watching the warm, flickering light. "Now, Bev, just relax," Harold said, "I'll call the company tomorrow and get the lights back on."

"Who's the dummy now?" I asked angrily. "Don't you know anything? Tomorrow's Saturday."

"Oh, I'm sorry. It is. I forgot. We have to think of selling the house," he said. "It'll take the pressure off. The economy has got to improve and we can always buy another house."

I couldn't believe my ears. The hospital and the house were the only homes I knew. "No, no," I screamed. "You can't sell this house. It's mine. It's mine."

"Quiet," he shook me by the shoulders. "It's ours. It's mine and yours. Do you think everything revolves around your precious skin? I live in it. I've wrecked my life and career looking after you. So shut up and think."

"I don't like you. You don't look after me. You just say you do."

I had struck a nerve, and Harold retaliated. I was a selfish and uncaring wife, he was sick of living with me, sick of taking care of me, tired of getting no rewards.

I reminded him that I had gotten home from the hospital and learned to cook immediately just to be a good wife.

"You think that's a reward?" he shouted. "I get better food in a restaurant. I'm talking about love. I'm talking about affection. I give you affection. You don't give me affection. I need a woman."

"I'm a woman," I shouted. "I *am* a woman. You just don't know what to do with a woman."

"I don't know?" he said. "I don't know?" He threw me down on some pillows, and holding both my hands with one of his, he undid the buttons of my jacket and blouse with the other.

"What are you doing?" I demanded, pretending I didn't know. "I'll never move. No, no, I won't!" I was trying to hit him with my fists but he held me off. "You're taking everything away from me. *My* house. *My* money."

"And I'm taking your virginity . . . "

The nerve! He wasn't asking or begging or coaxing or playing games anymore. Maybe I wasn't a virgin but I certainly was not going to give in to him—not ever again.

"I'll show you what you do with a woman," he growled. He was peeling off my clothes. I fought him off, but in spite of myself I was enjoying every minute. What a wonderful game!

"I'm cold. I want my clothes." But he ignored me, proceeding to arouse me in a way he had never done before. I didn't want him to stop, but I wasn't going to let him know it . . .

"This is rape," I said. "Help!"

"What do you know about rape?"

"Everything. I read the papers. Rape! *Rape!*"

I felt him enter me, and though he was still holding me captive, my hands above my head, I found myself moving with him. So this was what I had been missing. The climax was thrilling. Tenderly, he held me close. I started to laugh.

"What's so goddamn funny?"

"I'm naked and you have your clothes on." I giggled. "Did you like it the way I liked it?"

"Of course," he said.

"I know," I said. "I could feel you."

I couldn't stop laughing.

"Now what's funny?"

"Now I know what a virgin feels like on her wedding night."

"Fine. So now that you've had your honeymoon, woman, get me something to eat."

I threw on my clothes and we ran to the kitchen, gathering up things as fast as we could to get back to the fire. We ate hot dogs on rye bread slathered with mustard, some radishes, and skim milk.

"Best meal I ever had," he said, putting his head in my lap.

I wish that I could say we lived happily ever after, but the next morning dawned grim and cold and again we started fighting.

For some reason Harold did not want me to call Erma or Shirley or our children. Nor would he call. He didn't want anyone to know our predicament.

"I'll take care of it," was all he would say.

"But you don't take care of it," I shouted. All those phone calls about the bills were beginning to make sense. If you didn't respond, people did mean things.

"Do we still have a car, Harold?" I asked sarcastically.

"Yes, we still have a car. I did take care of that."

"Great."

"But I do need some cash for gas. How much do you have? We'll go get a few groceries tomorrow, if we have to."

I was crying as I looked in my purse. There were only a few dollars.

"What did you do with the money I gave you?" he said angrily.

"I went to the beauty parlor. You didn't tell me not to. I got my hair cut. Didn't you notice?"

"Yah, Yah, it's fine. I guess it's my own fault. I haven't leveled with you. I haven't told you what things are really like. I wanted you to enjoy things."

I didn't understand what he was talking about. It was so confusing—a lesson in poverty and fear. A lesson in humility. In insecurity.

I had thought the amnesia was my only problem. I had thought this man existed only to care for me and make sure I was safe. Now he was saying he should have ignored me and taken care of his business. What cruel turnabout was this?

Was it my fault? We would fight and make up, only to fight again. All the bitterness I felt about the insurance money came out . . .

"You signed. You knew what I was doing."

"No, I didn't understand. You didn't tell me."

"I was trying to make a better life for us. If it had worked, you would be singing a different tune. It was like trying to explain to a child. Could I help it if the economy was tough and I couldn't get orders?"

"Well, you kept saying you had orders."

"I did. I had some but not enough. And we shouldn't have moved to a bigger office. We should have stayed small."

"Should, should, should."

"And I shouldn't have given you all my attention. If I had stayed out on the road instead of running home to see how you were, I would have been better off. You don't even appreciate it. Listen to yourself."

"To hell with you. You took my money. I'm leaving."

"All right. But not until I give you something for the road." And again we were tussling . . .

"Damn it, woman, I think you like violent sex," Hal said afterward. "I'm going to have to start working out to be able to handle you. Where's the iodine?" He was nursing a scratch on his arm.

"Oh, poor baby," I cooed. "Let me kiss it."

"Just stay away from me," he laughed. "I need air." Seeing my dismay, he grabbed me. "Just kidding."

Soon we were fighting again—this time about whether to go to our children or friends for food and money. He refused. "We can survive one weekend. There's a lot of canned goods around here. I'll get some money Monday, somehow. And don't you have a check due from your new job?"

"I don't get it for another week," I said. "I don't think it's fair. If I work, I should keep my *own* money. You took all my insurance and I give you my work money. What's that all about?"

"It's called modern living. You read the papers. Don't you see where they say it takes two salaries to run a house these days? *You* even showed me a story."

"Well, I still want to know what happened to my money. *I* was supposed to get nineteen thousand dollars and I didn't get *anything*. I had the accident and I had all the pain and I didn't get anything."

"Do you want me to explain what happened? You never would listen. Are you ready to listen now, my friend?"

"Yes, my *friend*, I'd like to know exactly what happened to *my* money. My insurance money."

Bitterly, he explained how he and Butch had formed a partnership on just a handshake. No papers had been signed. "I trusted Butch and he trusted me," Hal said. "I still think he's an honest man. It just was the wrong time. And he didn't tell me his business was already in trouble. I thought I was just helping him expand. We were going to grow as a home improvement company. And we shouldn't have taken that big, expensive office. We wanted a good image, a good front. We weren't ready for that. We should have stayed small."

I sat curled up before the fire, listening. I was seeing a different side of my husband. He had always seemed so sure of himself. Now I realized that like me, he was trying to act more sure of himself than he really felt. I felt sorry for him. It was a new feeling for me.

Really listening and learning about business practices was a new experience for me, too. At first the partner had given Harold a certain amount of money every week—not a salary, but a draw against his sales.

"That's funny," I said. "He was giving you back some of your own money."

"Exactly," said Hal. "But after a while he couldn't afford even that. All the money he was taking in had to go back into the business. I lived on what little business I got—the commissions on it—and I used up our savings."

"Why didn't you get more business?"

"The economy is bad for home improvements. People are making do, using their money for food and basics. And the worse the economy, the crabbier people are when you do sell them on having a job done. They know they have you over a barrel and they want the sun and the moon. A couple of people threatened to sue and we had to do their jobs over again, and one man did take us to court."

"I'm sorry," I said. "You didn't make me understand."

"I didn't want you to worry. And all the times I rushed home to see how you were and whether you had set the house on fire, I really should have been out hustling. It's my own fault, I know, but I couldn't concentrate on work with you on my mind. You could wander off. You could get lost. You could go with some stranger—you were so gullible."

"Not that gullible. I'm a big girl now."

"Oh, now, sure. But who was running out the door?"

"That Bev is gone."

"Thank God. If I'm going to pull myself up again, I have to quit playing nursemaid. People have no patience with a man who's playing nursemaid. At first I would explain about you but then I learned it was just better to keep quiet. They have contempt for a man who runs around being worried about his wife all day. They don't think he can be much of a businessman."

"But everyone says you used to do very well."

"Oh, yes, before the accident. And didn't I tell you, the day of the accident, I was walking around with a big wad of money and a check for a big job? I was going to use the money for our trip to Jamaica. I felt on top of the world."

"I'm sorry your dream is gone."

"No, that was *your* dream."

"I'm sorry."

"Don't be sorry. You were walking with the light. You couldn't help it that a driver didn't see you."

"I should have been wearing bright colors. Red. Then he'd have seen me. Boy, everybody's going to see me from now on."

He kissed me. "Whatever love is," he said, "I guess I love you."

"Whatever love is," I echoed, "I guess I love you, too."

"Stop," he said dryly, "this great show of passion is more than I can take."

"Why didn't you go?" I asked. "Why do you stay with me when I've been so, as you say, 'unreasonable'?"

He looked at me. "I guess in our families, yours and mine, we just don't desert the ship."

Several times during that long weekend the phone rang and Harold would grab it. I realized he was afraid that if *I* answered, I would blurt out our problem and ask for money.

"Oh, we're just relaxing in front of the fire," I heard him say.

"Who was that?" I asked.

"That was Bob Wolf. They're going away for the weekend. He wants to get together next week."

"I'll bet we could go over there and stay in their nice warm house."

"Bev, I am not running anywhere. We are staying right here and we will handle this ourselves. We have plenty of food. We have plenty of wood, thank God. Do you realize the pioneers had only fireplaces to heat their houses and they had to cook over them, too? And they didn't have insulation like we have. So count your blessings."

"Yeah, that's what you always want me to do—shut up and count my blessings."

"Well, if you can't do the second part, at least do the first part."

"Ah, you told me to shut up! I'm going to leave you!"

Later I asked, "Did your folks send you to college?"

"No, my grandfather did. We had a shoe store and you know, he's about the one person I never worked for. Strange."

I was jealous of his sister. "Sometimes I think you like Elaine more than you like me."

"Don't be silly. It's an altogether different thing." He had always had a special protective older-brother attitude toward his sister. "When she went on a date, I always seemed to be up waiting for her when she came home. None of my friends would date her because of me. I was a mean S.O.B. when it came to her."

"Well, how did she manage to get married?"

"It's a funny thing—I didn't know who she was dating but she was dating someone and getting interested. And when she finally brought him home, it was someone I knew—Marvin Garfinkle—and she married him. Can you imagine? In spite of me, she ended up dating an acquaintance." Hal had been a responsible kid from the start, always working. "But I really found my own niche when I went into home improvements. I like to see a home grow more beautiful. I like everything about it and I'm a damned good salesman."

"I know," I said.

"How do you know?"

"My father says so."

"Good old dad. He's on my side."

"He says you've put up with a lot since my accident and I should try to be nice to you."

"He's so right. You should."

"I'm trying, Harold."

"Okay. I'm waiting."

"For what?"

"For you to finish growing up."

I wondered if I ever would. I wondered if I wanted to. I wondered how grown-up Hal was if he could forget to pay the light and heat bills. He had said it was because he was so upset and worried about me and he didn't have the money—but I wondered.

Now, beside the warming fire, with Hal's arms around me, I heard the full story of his life. How wonderful his childhood had been and how much fun he and I had had after we started going together. Dancing had been our thing. I had studied tap dancing and my father had made a fine ballroom dancer of me. That surprised me.

"I didn't know I studied dancing. You mean my mother sent me to a dancing school?"

"She sure did. From the time you were seven, but I didn't know you then."

"Maybe I should have been on the stage."

"You were too shy. But you sure were a fine dancer on stage when my lodge had a show and you were in the chorus."

"Nobody told me."

"Yes, they did. Remember the gal we met on the street who said, 'Don't you remember, Beverly, we danced in the show together?' "

"Oh, I didn't know that was what she meant."

"You just cut her off by saying, 'No.' You should draw people out when they recognize you and try to tell you how they know you. Ask questions. Don't cut them off."

"But you get tired when I ask you too many questions."

"I'm not talking about me. I'm talking about strangers. Ask them. They're really not strangers. They know you."

"Okay, I'll try. But they make me feel so dumb. They look at me so strangely."

"Well, look at it from their viewpoint for a change. How would you feel if the person you did things with now acted as if she'd never seen you before?"

Hal had first set eyes on me on the beach at Atlantic City. I was with some girls. He was with some fellows.

"Why did you choose me?" I asked.

"I didn't choose you right then. A fellow who knew you introduced you and I was impressed enough to ask you for a date for that night."

"Why were you impressed?"

"I was impressed with your black one-piece bathing suit and the figure inside. You were built right—and you still are. Men have an expression for it that I'm sure you don't remember but it's too coarse, too vulgar to tell you. I'm trying to get you to leave off rough talk and talk like a lady."

So that was how he'd met me. On the beach. And it hadn't been my brain but my body that had attracted him.

"Did you take me to a movie and dinner and dancing?"

"Are you crazy? I was broke. I was a kid. I think we both were about seventeen. I guess I got you a hot dog and we sat on the boardwalk and smooched a little. That means kissing like this."

But I didn't want more kisses. I wanted information. How did we get from sitting on the boardwalk to a honeymoon?

"Honeymoon? Is that what you call one night in a ten dollar a night hotel room with a big dollar tip to the bellboy to impress you? The real honeymoon was being together in bed with no one able to point a finger or say, 'Throw the bum out.' Honeymoon meant sex unlimited. Right in your father's house. Wow!"

"Didn't you mind living with my parents?"

"No, it's sort of family tradition in my family. My folks lived with in-laws, too, until they could afford their own home."

Hal said that after we married, while I worked for the dentist, he had worked at my uncle's lamp manufacturing plant. I was amazed to learn Hal was only six months older than I was.

"Did you graduate from college?" I asked.

"I wanted to, but I didn't. In fact, in my second year I gave it up for you."

"Why? You shouldn't have."

"You're so right. I must have been out of my mind. I had some silly notion that I wanted to be married."

"You did?" At last he was saying something almost sweet. "Because I was pretty?"

"I guess, and because we were both in heat. Do you want me to show you what that is?" He pushed me back against the pillows . . .

Afterward, laughing, he said, "You see how educational sex is? You're getting a whole new vocabulary."

"Is it all right for me to tell people we were both in heat?"

"Only Shirley and Erma—friends like that. *Animals* go into heat. If you want to say something along that line, say 'We were very romantic last night,' or something like that. You have to pretty it up. Animals have sex. People have romance. I mean, when they're talking about it. I'm sure you and the girls talk about it. It's natural."

"Do men talk about sex too? What do they say?"

"I'll tell you what they say. When I brought you home they kept kidding me and saying, 'How does it feel to have sex with a forty-eight-year-old virgin?' They were jealous as hell. They thought I was having some kind of Lolita orgy. I didn't have the heart to tell them."

"Tell them what?" I knew I wasn't going to like the answer.

"That it's like having sex with a three-year-old who's more interested in her dolls—in this case, panda—than what you're trying to do to her." He paused. "Thank God that's over, and now that you've mastered the basic course, we can go on to finer points."

"What's a finer point?"

"Oh, all kinds of things. Enjoyment of the body. You'll find out."

What more was there to find out? When I liked him, I responded. When I was angry with him, I didn't. It was as simple as that.

But I still had a lot to learn about our romance. After that first date, Harold hadn't seen me again for many months. He was in college and I was in high school. He went to Temple University in Philadelphia to study business administration.

"How old were we when we got married?"

"Let's see. I guess I was twenty and you were verging on it. The baby came practically as your first anniversary gift."

"Joanie thinks I resented being tied down so soon and so young."

"I won't dispute it. And maybe I resented being tied down so early, too. But there it is. And we made it and we'll make it. I'm feeling more cheerful about us."

"Me too," I said. "I like you lots better."

"I know it's natural to resent someone who's always the boss."

"I guess you were a little bit mad at me, too."

"A little bit? That's putting it mildly."

"Did you want to get a divorce?"

"I can honestly say I wasn't going that far. But I definitely was considering just getting away. Just grabbing a suitcase and going."

"Where? Where would you go?"

"Anywhere. California. Florida. Texas. New York. Someplace where I could be with adults, where I didn't have to be a babysitter."

"I'm sorry."

"You can't help it. But thank God, you're growing up. You're making sense. Even if you're mad now, you have good reason. Remember, when the insurance money came you were just a child. What good would it have done to get your opinion? What did you know about business?"

We sat looking at each other and I started to get mad again, thinking about the money he'd lost. He must have read my mind because he said, "Of course, I have to admit in all fairness that my own judgment was faulty, too. I really think I was so upset over what happened to you and the hell I was living through that I lost my good sense for a while. I think of it now and see all the mistakes and I can't believe I did it. I didn't check the man's credit—I assumed he was in good shape and was looking for just some chance to expand his business. Well, it turned out he wasn't in such good shape. I should have found out. I should have had a lawyer work out the terms of the partnership. I shouldn't have invested that much money on a handshake. It was a lapse of judgment. I should have this and I should have that."

"But you're okay now, aren't you? You don't owe him anything."

"Yeah, the one good point was that since I didn't sign papers I wasn't legally responsible, and even there I was so dumb I didn't have my own lawyer to tell me that. And I was still shelling out money based on what *his* lawyer said. If I hadn't called a halt to it, I might still be paying off the company's debts or paying for his bankruptcy."

When Harold came home on Monday he announced that he had gotten the money and ordered the light and gas restored immediately.

"That's good," I said. "Where did you get it?"

"I borrowed it."

"Oh, you went to the bank?"

"Yes, I went to the bank."

"We'll pay it back soon, won't we?"

"As soon as I can."

"You can use my money to pay it back."

"For the time being we need your salary for living expenses."

"Then how will we pay it back?"

"Look, will you let me handle it? Just as soon as I get some new business, I'll be getting in money. This is just a temporary thing. I made the loan and I'll pay for it and it's *my* business how I do it, not *yours*."

"All right, Harold." I felt humble. Somehow, it didn't sound right or fair, but I didn't know what else to do. I tried to tell myself that the lights would go back on and all would be right with the world.

But Little Beverly had her own opinion. "Here we go again," she whispered to me. "I don't like being grown-up anymore. Let's go somewhere where nobody ever has to be grown-up." I listened and then put her away again, back in the secret place deep inside me. I had better not listen. It was time to stay grown-up.

Afterwards, I could not resist telling Erma what had happened. She told her husband, Bob, who had called Harold and asked why he hadn't tried to borrow from him.

I thought Hal would be angry, but he wasn't. "You couldn't help it dear. You're still my child bride. As you grow up, you'll learn to keep secrets."

But there was something worse, something that wasn't a secret—the For Sale sign on the lawn. Thinking about it made me cry. How I hated seeing it every morning! I asked Harold if I could pull it out.

"No, dear. That's part of growing up, too. You have to learn to put the past behind you. Put your mind on the lovely apartment you are going to have and how much less work you will have taking care of it."

"Will I still have flowers outside?"

"Well, they will probably be outside but you won't be permitted to dig around in them. We'll try to find an apartment that looks out on flowers."

"But that won't be the same," I said, close to tears. "I want to plant my little flowers in the ground and pull out the weeds."

So the sign stood outside, taunting me, and soon a procession of strangers began to march through the house. My house. I hoped it never sold. Meanwhile, to prepare for the move, Hal kept taking me to see different apartment houses, each more depressing than the last.

And that's where Christmas, 1981, found me—sitting in the car, crying, refusing to get out and look at my prospective new home.

15

A Cry for Help

I was going to lose my house, I had almost lost my husband—and might still—and now I was confronted by a whole new spectrum of money worries. I only *thought* my life was on an even keel—obviously I still had a lot of growing up to do. And if facing such things was being grown-up, what was the good of it? Maybe I should be Little Bev forever.

Little Bev started coming out more and more. "I don't care," she said, "I'm not going to pay attention to anybody. I'm mad. I'm scared. I don't like being grown-up."

In January, 1982, Harold and I spent a week at the Institute of Living, in Hartford, Connecticut, to have tests and sessions with a psychiatrist, Dr. Raymond Veeder.

I noticed immediately that Dr. Veeder had a slight foreign accent. Somehow that made me feel more comfortable about opening up to him about myself, my life, my loneliness, and my anger.

I hated to tattle on Harold about the money, but that was what I was there for, wasn't it? To talk about what was bothering me and how I was making out? Maybe I would even find out what my future held—and whether my memory would return.

Dr. Veeder asked if he could talk to Harold alone. I said I didn't mind, but in my heart I wished I could listen in. That first afternoon he and Harold talked for an hour.

Then, afterward, I saw Dr. Veeder again, and he gave me a test in which he told me proverbs and I was to give their meaning. I didn't know if he liked my answers or not, but one of the proverbs made me cry and I wouldn't respond—it was something about the tongue or a big mouth being the enemy of the neck. At the time I wasn't quite sure what it was about it that bothered me—but looking back, I guess it was the fact that it reminded me of the accident and the fracture of the skull right above my own neck.

I seemed to spend a lot of time crying in my sessions with Dr. Veeder, maybe because my life sounded so sad as I heard myself recounting the facts. But even as I cried, it was such a relief to be able to tell my story—all of it—to someone who seemed so sympathetic, someone who listened and wouldn't get angry at me.

I had many tests. One was an EEG—an electroencephalographic test—and I went through the first part with no problem. But when the barbiturate they gave me for the second part of the test didn't work, the rest of the test was canceled.

Every time I turned around, or so it seemed, they tried a new test on me.

Bender-Gestalt Test; Trail Making Test; Aphasia Screening Test (I remember I couldn't pronounce Massachusetts and a few other words); Rorschach Test (I kept saying, "I see a center line with spots on it and an inkblot that's lighter in some places, darker in other places." I did not know then the variety of animals and things and even motions that some people see in those ink blots.); Minnesota Multiphasic Personality Inventory; and Wechsler Adult Intelligence Scale.

Dr. Veeder didn't tell me the results. I would have hated to have to show Harold a report that confirmed that his wife was a dummy.

On the last day Harold and I met with Dr. Veeder to discuss all our problems—especially the money problems.

I was shocked to learn that Harold had gotten the money for our electric bills from his father.

"You said you got it from the bank," I said angrily.

"No, I didn't. You assumed it and I let you believe it. I got turned down at the bank. I had no choice."

"You said you didn't want anyone to know. You wouldn't let *me* tell anyone. You made me stay in the cold because you didn't want the family to know."

"I said I had no choice, finally."

"How much did you borrow?"

"A thousand dollars."

"That's lots more than the bills were!" I was furious. I didn't care if the doctor heard. Let him see what life was like in our house!

"We had to live. Food, gas for the car, and it was a while till your next paycheck. And you didn't want the gas to be turned off again, did you? He knows I'll pay him back."

"But how can you borrow from your *father*? He's retired. He needs his money."

"You see, doctor, how she carries on, worrying about everyone but me?" I let that go by. Maybe I deserved it. Anyway, I felt better when Harold said he had paid off some of our debts. And I also felt better seeing that he did care about me and hadn't wanted me to worry. Maybe there was hope for us after all.

Dr. Veeder seemed to think so. He recommended that we continue having joint sessions with someone nearer home. Now I realized I hadn't told him about Little Beverly. I didn't know why.

It was over. I had survived.

As we walked around the beautiful grounds of the Institute of Living, we felt like honeymooners. We discussed going into therapy together. "Let's just wait until I get my business problems stabilized and can afford it," Harold said. "That fifty or seventy-five dollars a week is just one burden too many right now. There's an old proverb about the straw that broke the camel's back."

"Please," I said, "no proverbs now."

A few weeks after we got home, I received a letter from Dr. Veeder in which he said that my amnesia was partly organic, partly psychological. One sentence stood out in my mind: "It is possible that with psychotherapy you may be able to resolve much of your amnesia although, in all probability, you will never achieve recall of events immediately prior to and immediately following the accident, since this part of your amnesia is organic."

He reiterated his suggestion that Harold and I seek help together, "because so much has happened in both your lives since the accident and with such rapidity that it has been quite difficult for both of you to make the necessary adjustment."

"Well," said Harold, "what do you want to do?"

"What do you want to do?" I countered.

"I don't want to do anything till I get out of debt and am financially solvent and on my feet. But the important thing is what do you want to do?"

"I don't know."

"Considering that it might help you get part of your memory back . . . How badly do you want to remember?"

"Sometimes very badly. Would I still be me and have my job?"

"I don't know if you would lose *this* you. You should have asked him."

"I don't know. The girls at CETA need me. They can't get it all from a book. They're supposed to read the chapter and take the test and that's all but that's not enough. I explain all kinds of things to them."

"That's very noble. Are you sure that's all you're worried about?"

"I'm worried about me, too. I feel I would just go poof and disappear. Everything I know would disappear. I don't want to talk about it."

"Well, it's up to you. It's your money, as you like to point out. If you feel it's important to go for therapy, we'll manage somehow."

"How much does it cost?"

"Depends on the man. Fifty or seventy-five dollars is rock-bottom for one person and I don't know what it is for seeing two people together. And I guess your sessions for getting your memory back would be separate from our marriage counseling. I have no idea on cost. I hear some psychiatrists charge one hundred dollars a shot these days."

"I don't think I want to do it right now. I'd rather wait till after we sell the house and see how I feel. Suddenly I just don't know how important it is to remember. I'm accepting you now as my husband and all the rest of the family I can understand. I'm used to everyone now. And we're happier now that we've talked to Dr. Veeder."

He kissed me. "I know I am."

"I am, too. Was it Dr. Veeder or that other man who said, 'Love is trust.' I trust you more now."

"That's good, honey. And I've always trusted you, even though you've been a little headache to me sometimes."

"I know."

Now Harold seemed to want to talk about *his* previous psychiatric experience. He had thought a woman psychologist would be more sympathetic and better able to explain me to him.

"Did she explain me?"

"Not much. She was too busy explaining about herself. I kept telling her how it felt to be told your wife might be a vegetable and how I brought home this child from the hospital who was like a Mexican jumping bean and made little sense. And she kept telling me about her husband who had been terminally ill for a long time and how she had had to cope with it.

"I said, 'Look, doctor, I'm hurting. I'm falling behind in my work. I don't know what to do. I don't know how to survive.'

"She said, 'My husband died and I coped with it. And I'm doing very well, see? I didn't lose a day of work all that time.'

"I said, 'Congratulations!' and I got up and started to walk out. She yelled after me, 'Wait. Are you coming back?' and I said, 'Send me your bill. You've got the address.' "

"And you never went back?"

"Nope. I figured she ought to hire her own psychologist to listen to her talk about herself."

"Why didn't you go to someone else?"

"Money, of course. It's a luxury item. Everybody needs a little help—more or less. I figured I'd find my own answers. I didn't hear anything from her that I didn't already know."

"Oh."

I felt sure that I could handle my own life, too. I realized that it wasn't Harold's responsibility to make me happy. He hadn't really been able to handle his own life. No, it was up to me to find out what I wanted—and make it happen.

But I was glad he was there. He was in every sense my husband. At last.

Now that I was a real woman, with a woman's sexuality, I felt much more relaxed and at ease. Life was more pleasant and so was Harold. But something else bothered me. I wanted to look more like my daughter. I wanted to look younger, prettier.

I complained about it to my buddies at lunch. "I don't like my face. I don't like the lines beside my nose. I don't like the way my eyelids droop." Erma and Shirley chuckled.

"Well, tough luck," they said. "You've finally noticed that you're past the first flush of youth. We *all* are. White it out with makeup or see your plastic surgeon."

Ah, plastic surgeon. I knew what that was. I would look it up in my medical books or I'd look it up in the library. We went to the restroom and they showed me how I would look if the skin of my cheeks was pulled back to get rid of the puffiness and the droop.

The three of us stood admiring the new Bev in the huge mirror. I loved it.

"I've got to tell Harold about this," I said as soon as we got back to our table.

"I wouldn't," they said. "You'd better break it to him gently."

"He's been through an awful lot," said one.

"He's already done his hospital duty," said the other.

"Okay, okay," I said. "I get the picture. I'd better figure this thing out and try some tact."

"She's growing," said one.

"She's getting positively sophisticated," said the other.

My heart sang. *Me*—sophisticated! Finally they could see it.

I didn't tell Harold about it until I had seen the plastic surgeon. In fact, I saw *two* plastic surgeons. I don't know why, but I didn't like the first one, so I simply thanked him for telling me what he would do with my face and marched out.

"I've decided to have a face lift," I said one day.

"What?"

"I'm going to give you a younger wife."

"Thanks, but I'll keep the one I have."

"But you want a happy wife, don't you?"

"What do I have to pay for a happy wife?"

"Something like three thousand dollars. A fair cut of the sale of the house and the insurance money I gave up when I was a dummy. Fair enough?" I thought we'd have a real knock-down, drag-out fight, but rather quickly he capitulated, saying with a sigh, "Anything for a happy wife, I guess."

Tact had not yet become a part of my daily life. I still had a tendency to say whatever popped into my mind, and I still stopped strangers whenever or wherever I felt like it.

One day I saw a man on the street who fitted to a T Harold's description of a homosexual. I walked over to him and asked, "Are you gay?" He just stared—first at me, then at Harold.

But Harold was walking away from me as if he didn't know me. Without answering, the man quickly turned and walked into the nearest building.

When I had caught up with Hal, he said, "You don't ask that question of someone you don't even know."

"Why? It's not a cuss word."

"No, it's not a cuss word. It's a matter of tact. I thought I told you. I haven't got time to explain it now. You run into the food market while I go to the bank and I'll be back to help you finish up at the check-out counter. Try not to get into a discussion with everyone in the aisles—I don't have time for it."

My students were my lifeline. I needed them even more than they needed me. I loved teaching. But one thing bothered me— there was no practical experience for the girls supposedly training to help doctors. It was all theoretical. There were no actual doctors' offices they could examine, no items they might be called on to use, such as blood pressure cuffs, stethoscopes, or even thermometers.

I went to the director with my complaint.

By now she knew about my amnesia. Apparently someone I had confided in had told her. But I was all business. "How can they learn to use these things without handling them and using them? I have to show them how the equipment works and have them do it."

"Well," she said, "if you're willing to bring your own instruments . . ."

"I am. I am."

" . . . then I can let you use a room downstairs once a week. You can take them down in little groups to show them so they don't disturb the rest of the class, who are studying."

I wanted to argue that it would be good for the rest of the class to watch and listen, but I remembered tact and bit my tongue. I was winning, wasn't I?

I didn't think the measly forty minutes a week was enough. I took only six girls at a time and each girl had to round up subjects to work on—other students who were between classes. I would then check their findings. Meanwhile, an aide would watch over my class upstairs.

As I presided over my class, I would think, *These poor girls are disadvantaged and even their school is disadvantaged.*

I couldn't stand it. I knew Harold was having terrible financial problems, I knew it wasn't practical . . . but in protest, I quit the job.

Later, I heard the course was discontinued. I wasn't surprised.

It was only after I had burned my bridges behind me that I realized I may have been a bit impetuous. Harold was still depressed, going from job to job. For a time he tried to sell telephone services to businesses. Leads that he had been promised didn't materialize, and those that did led to nothing. I had no choice—I applied for unemployment benefits.

I yearned for something to work toward. Something that would assure me that my life was worthwhile. Yes, I was learning to be an adult—but I was an adult without a past, a failure . . . not once, but *twice.* The knowledge hurt.

———————

"Mr. Slater told me how he tended to protect his wife from any problems, financial or otherwise, which arose and, as he continued talking, it seemed that most of the problems that he protected her from were all financial so that, when she learned by accident that the financial situation of the family was serious, she was unable to cope with it, became extremely upset and tearful and eventually resentful of her husband."

VI

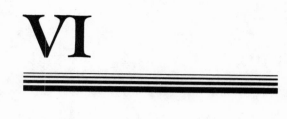

TO LIVE AGAIN

16

The Human Dynamo

I was going to do it all. By myself. I was going to be my own psychiatrist, analyze my needs, set goals, feel fulfilled. And oh, yes, I would cope with that Other Image. I didn't have to be everything she was. I didn't want to.

I felt much more confident now, much more a complete person. I decided to look at my life from a different angle. I'd had two jobs in which people depended upon me. It had been so nice to feel wise.

But something was missing. What else did I need? More friends. A feeling of achievement. And like Rodney Dangerfield, more respect.

I was ready to face the world and get what I needed. So why was I sitting at home, still studying my old medical books?

Somehow I couldn't adjust. I couldn't bear it when things weren't done my way. Would I have been fired from the school had I not quit?

Confident or not, I was adrift in a world of strangers. I wanted to explain myself, to have people know the way it felt.

I decided to take the initiative. I called a local TV talk show and was invited to appear, along with my family. The show was to be filmed at my house. Harold and Stuart were less than thrilled, Stuart absolutely refusing to go under scrutiny as "part of a freak show." It took considerable arm twisting to get him to agree.

How exciting it was! The swarms of technicians, the cheerful talk-show hosts. I had never felt more alive, more real than when I was under the bright lights, all attention focused on me.

Then I felt sure. *Then* I felt smart. I was the only one who could answer their questions. But my hopes that it would lead to lasting friendships were dashed—when the show was over, it really *was* over.

"I'll bet some magazine would tell my story," I said to Harold one night. "I'll bet if I called a magazine, they would write my story."

"Don't be ridiculous," he said. "Who cares about someone else's amnesia?"

"Everyone."

I would show him. I was through asking for opinions and permission. I spent the next day on the phone, calling one magazine after another, learning a little more each time about how to deal with editors.

They didn't seem to believe me. They would take my telephone number and say they would have to call me back. Some asked if I had a writer, some if I had a press agent. I assured them I just wanted everyone to know how it felt to be adrift in a world where everyone else seemed to belong.

"How does it feel?" one editor asked.

"Lonely," I told her, "like there is no bottom to the loneliness and a feeling that there must be somewhere else that you belong."

I didn't tell Harold about my plan. There'd be time enough later, when the phone bill came. By then I'd think of something to say in my defense.

Harold came home disgusted. "I've been trying to call home all day. What happened? Did you die with the phone at your ear?"

"Something like that," I said. "It's been a fun day." I didn't tell him what I had been up to until the next day—the phone rang so often it almost jumped off the wall. Almost *everyone* phoned back but I felt it was only fair I tell my story to the first magazine who called back—*Ladies' Home Journal*. Besides, I liked the way the editor sounded—so amazed and sympathetic. It was a little overwhelming to be suddenly in such demand.

Not until Norman Schreiber, the writer assigned to my story, arrived for the interview would Harold believe that there were people all over the country who were interested in my amnesia.

The article gave me fresh confidence. But the rest of my life was still in trouble. My new resolve to control my life, it seemed, could extend only so far.

After looking at countless apartments, Hal had eventually decided on a complex of apartment buildings with large rooms, lovely balconies, beautifully landscaped and it wasn't too expensive. We could buy or rent.

"I'm not emotionally ready to get boxed in again with mortgage payments and down payments," Harold said. "I need the cushion of money in the bank for us to live comfortably." And so we applied for a rental apartment and were put on a waiting list.

When the house was sold, we were told we had to be out by May. The only apartment available was on the tenth floor of Landmark II. I noticed the number on the door and cringed—1013. Could I never get away from that terrible number thirteen? Already the apartment felt hexed. But I didn't dare tell Hal, who was happily going through the rooms, exclaiming on their size and pointing out that the second bedroom would make a fine family-TV-study room. "And look at this balcony," he called. "Beverly, come out here and see."

I walked toward the sliding glass doors and stopped. "I can't," I said. "I can't look down." I knew that if I had to live there, I would never set foot on that balcony.

"My God," he said, "you're the same as you ever were. The amnesia hasn't changed you."

"I can't help it," I said. "I can't live here. It's too high up. How will I use the elevator when you're not here?"

"You can call the doorman to come get you. But I'll be here a lot and I'll take you."

"No, I can't live here."

"I'm sorry. We can change apartments later but I've got to get in now because the house deal is ready for settlement."

I was ready to cry again but Harold hugged me and told me how lucky we were to have such a nice, airy place to live. "And did you see the flowers downstairs around the shrubbery? You wanted flowers, didn't you?"

"Yes," I said, "but they don't do me any good from up here."

And so we moved in. But it wasn't easy. Unless someone was waiting for the elevator on my floor, I would walk down all ten flights. Then I started buzzing for the elevator until one arrived with someone already in it. And no matter what Harold did, I wasn't satisfied. I wanted new rugs and he let me pick wall-to-wall carpeting throughout the rooms. I complained that the family room had no cabinets, as our house had, and he ordered custom-built cabinets. I said the kitchen looked too white, like the hospital, and he took me shopping for colorful wallpaper.

"Just look in the Yellow Pages and call a paperhanger," he said. I hid the wallpaper in a closet and did not call the paperhanger. Finally, exasperated, he confronted me. "What do you want?"

"To get out of here."

"Be patient," he said. "Wait till business picks up. Wait till I'm in better shape financially, and then you know what we're going to do?"

"No," I said. "I'm afraid to find out."

"I've got my eye on some garden-style condominium apartments that are being built. There are flowers galore and you'll walk right out of your front door into your flower garden. I'll even sit in my lawn chair and watch you garden." He was grinning.

"Oh, that makes me so happy," I said. "I'd love that. When can we look?"

"Right now. But first you must promise to be a good girl and not complain about living here anymore."

"I promise, I promise."

But it was hard living in this place while I waited for our dream house to come true. I tried to focus on my life outside those four walls . . .

When people heard that I was going to be written up in *Ladies' Home Journal*, they thought I was now into a new phase of my development—that I had changed from willful child to publicity-mad teenager. But they were wrong. And I was afraid to tell them that I needed other people in my life.

I yearned to have people write and say they understood. They did. "Hang on," they wrote. "We're with you."

How I wished Harold would say "I admire you so for fighting your way back. Thanks for sharing your experience."

Harold thanked me if I *didn't* share my experience. "Can you just leave off?" he would warn me before we went visiting. "Can you just give it a rest?"

And I would. But I would pout in a corner, not really coming to life until someone asked me about my amnesia.

I read the newspapers and tried to prepare myself for conversations on the news of the day, like Hal did, but somehow I could never remember what to say to get started.

Suddenly I got the phone call I had been waiting for—from someone who really knew about amnesia from personal experience. Her name was Renée, she lived in Rochester, Minnesota, and she was a young woman— only thirty-five—who had been in a traffic accident that had completely wiped out her memory.

Renée had been comatose for four or five days. When she woke up, the faces around her looked familiar but they had no names. She couldn't remember colors and had lost a great deal of her vocabulary, as I had, but she was even worse off in that she could not remember numbers either.

There was so much I wanted to know. How had it happened? When had it happened to her? We couldn't believe it—both of us had had our accidents on the thirteenth! And on Wednesdays, too. Wednesday, May 13, 1981 was her date.

"You read how it happened to me," I said, "tell me, tell me quick, what happened to you. I can hardly wait to find out, Renée."

"It's a lot like yours, Beverly. I was on my moped on the way to nursing school when someone in a parked car opened the door and I rammed into it. Then I bounced and flew into the traffic lane and was hurled to the hood of another car. Do you remember anything about your accident?"

"Nothing. I don't even remember that I was on my way to work and crossing the street."

Renée had good news for me. Little by little, her memory had been returning, and she remembered everything about her accident. On that day she got on her moped, as usual, for the five-mile sprint to her class at Rochester Community College. She was not wearing her helmet. The driver of the car whose hood she'd landed on was a licensed practical nurse, and she had started resuscitating Renée before the ambulance arrived. If the nurse hadn't been there, Renée would have died.

So in that regard, too, we were alike—both of us had been pulled back from death.

But Renée was luckier—*she* was remembering. "Now strange

little things about my childhood are coming back to me, Beverly. Has anything come back to you? Anything about when you were little?"

"Nothing about being little, nothing about being big. You can't imagine how I envy you."

I couldn't bear to hang up. At last I had a friend who knew, who understood, who sympathized. The next call revealed more similarities. Renée's personality had changed, too.

Before the accident she had been introverted, and now she was gregarious—she had even become involved in a theater group.

"I can't contain myself either," I said. "I find myself going over to strangers at their tables in restaurants and just talking to them. My family hates it. I can confess to you that this thing hasn't helped my marriage."

She shared this experience as well. Apparently even before the accident she and her husband had started seeing a marriage counselor; and they had decided to get a divorce.

I told Renée about my temper tantrums when I first came home from the hospital, how I would run out of the house and Harold would have to follow me to see that I didn't wander into traffic or get lost. Renée understood. "I would hit myself or pound my fist on the wall or on a table," she said, "and ended up with bruises and broken blood vessels, I hit so hard."

But this letting go of anger had been beneficial for each of us— my blood pressure had dropped and her spastic colon condition had almost disappeared.

Renée said that her psychiatrist had been a great help to her. "Sometimes I would feel that I was going insane, thinking and knowing I was different—trying to get other people to realize that I was different. Unless they had suffered brain damage themselves, other people could never fully understand . . . "

That was exactly how I felt. I told her that some good had come of my accident because friends seemed to like the new me better.

Renée said that her accident had also brought its rewards . . . by introducing her to the wife of a rabbi, Suanne Fried Goodman, who had become a great friend and was responsible for bringing the article about me to Renée's attention; as well as David Fellman, the treasurer of the synagogue, with whom she had started a romance.

He wanted to marry her. Would it be fair to him, she wondered? I was thrilled that she was asking my opinion. Judging by the way she talked about him and the things she said—evidently he was compassionate and understanding—I said, yes, yes, yes.

Renée was also concerned about how a new marriage would affect her children, one of whom was quite young. Could she impose *another* stranger on them?

I told Renée about how my two children had reacted to the new Beverly.

"Take a chance, Renée," I said. "Somehow it all works out. At first, I didn't want to live in a house with my husband, either. He was a stranger. I didn't even know whether I liked him. And now I love every day. Take a chance."

Soon after, Renée did marry, as I knew she would, and she and David and her three children— Julie, Joe, and Andrew—moved into a new house.

I continued to receive letters after the appearance of the *Ladies' Home Journal* article. A psychic wrote that she was sure my body was being used by another spirit—that would explain why I did not recognize anybody and why I knew nothing of my former life.

Timidly, I showed Harold the letter, sure he would pooh-pooh it. He sighed and said that he didn't know anything about psychics but he didn't think I could handle trying to find out what creature was inhabiting my body.

"Who knows what's possible?" I said.

"Right. I don't know what's possible. I don't think anybody on earth knows. You could speculate endlessly."

"Do you think I should answer the letter?"

"Not if you don't want to get involved. Where does the psychic live?"

I looked at the letterhead. "California."

"What did she call you?"

"A 'walk-in.' Maybe when people are dying someone can step into their bodies and keep them alive— except then they're someone else."

"Well, you are certainly *someone else,* but I don't buy the walk-in theory. I think someday you're going to remember the real you.

I mean, the original you. At least part of her. Well, are you going to answer her?"

"I don't know. I have to think about it." After several days of brooding about the letter, I suddenly realized something: I didn't want to know. I didn't want to get involved.

But I did want to be involved in something else, something much more cheerful . . .

Stuart was getting married.

It was my first wedding in my new life. I would not only be a guest—I would be an *honored* guest. Mother of the groom. I would wear a special dress. I would stand with the bride and groom under the canopy of flowers.

"You've hit the jackpot on this one, my dear," Harold said. "I think Stuart is going to make history with his half-and-half wedding. This is surely going to make up for all the weddings you missed."

"Neither of us is going to give up his religion," Stuart said. "We want a more modern approach, so we're going to have two religious ceremonies taking place simultaneously at our wedding, with a rabbi and a priest officiating."

"Your father says you're making history."

"I'm not doing it to make history. I'm just trying to make sense. You wouldn't be offended, would you, at the dual-religion ceremony?"

"Of course not," I said. "You know how I feel about religion. I feel something about God but I can't feel anything but confused about religion."

I watched with joy as a priest and rabbi conducted the ceremony. Mari's parents sat in the front row, as was the Catholic custom, and Harold and I stood with our son, as was the Jewish custom. Mari lit the candles. Stuart crushed a glass underfoot.

We all signed a book that showed that this unique wedding had taken place on August 28, 1982. Afterward many people came up to say they had read about me in the *Ladies' Home Journal* the month before. One woman invited me to come speak at her club. "Everyone is so curious about amnesia."

I no longer had to call TV stations—they called me.

I went to Detroit, Chicago, San Francisco, and a few other towns—usually without Harold. In the green room of one television studio I met Rex Reed and asked, "Are you gay?"

He just looked at me and said, "Nobody has ever asked that question before in all the years I've been appearing on talk shows." Everyone else in the room looked shocked. I started to apologize, but he just laughed.

When I told Harold about this little incident, he shook his head and said, "I thought we'd been through this before. I thought you agreed you don't ask this question of strangers."

"But he wasn't a stranger. I was introduced."

In Detroit, my room in the hotel was on the twentieth floor. I was terrified. How was I going to get downstairs every day? I couldn't possibly walk down all those stairs. And room service was too lonely.

I tried my elevator trick. It didn't work—every car that came along was empty. I was tired, lonely, and frustrated.

Little Beverly took over. I walked back to my room, and, chuckling like a naughty child, I picked up the phone and said haughtily to the operator, "My dear, I have a problem. I have a large amount of cash that I dare not leave in my room. I must have a security officer to escort me to the dining room. Can you arrange it?"

She could. She did. And when I was finished eating, the security man was hovering nearby, ready to take me back to my room. It amazed me how people love to do favors for someone they think is walking around with a bundle of money. Loving every minute of my new role, I tipped him handsomely.

By far, my most exciting TV adventure was being on the "Fantasy" program, hosted by Leslie Uggams in Los Angeles.

Leslie told the audience about my dream of one day visiting Jamaica. Now, she announced, my fantasy was going to become reality—"Fantasy" was sending Harold and me to Jamaica.

I still can feel the thrill of those words. At last, something wonderful was happening. Somewhere in my old preaccident papers, I had found the line "And God fulfills Himself in many ways." Now I knew it was true. But I vowed to know why I had this fixation on Jamaica . . .

"What difference does it make?" Harold asked. "Let's just say it was someplace you wanted to go because you had never been there."

Maybe when I saw Jamaica, I would know.

And so, on the third anniversary of my accident—February 13, 1983—I found myself on an airplane heading for my dream vacation. I was very nervous. But Harold was beside me and as another poem I had found said, "All's right with the world."

17

Full Circle

So this was Jamaica.

In my Other Image days, I had been to plenty of sun-drenched spots—Acapulco, Puerto Rico, and Trinidad.

So why this obsession with Jamaica? I still wondered aloud.

"Maybe you developed a yen for the British West Indies," Harold said. "Jamaica is part of the British West Indies, and so is Trinidad. How do I know how a woman's mind works? Especially yours. You weren't much of a communicator. You didn't tell me why you were carrying Fayne's number around. Why? Why this? Why that? You could go crazy asking why about a lot of things. It happens and that's it."

"I wish I could be like you," I said. "I wish I didn't want to know."

We landed. Now I was in my fantasy land.

Beauty was all around me. The colors of the rainbow, huge exotic flowers. It was like being back in the tunnel between life and death. But this was life. I looked at the waters. They were still, no waves rippling toward me, the way they had at Atlantic City. I walked into the water and looked down at my feet. No, this was definitely not like Atlantic City. This water was so clear and, from the shore, so green. Everything was green. Except for the flowers —purples, reds, and vibrant yellows. And the trees on the beach. I did not know there *could* be trees on a beach.

I wanted to spend a day on the beach outside our hotel, but there was so much to do and to see! We promised ourselves that we would save it for our last day, when we were limp from exhaustion.

We enjoyed long, idyllic days. The sand was whiter than anything I'd ever seen.

But all was not bliss on my dream vacation . . .

You had to get on the beach before 9:00 A.M. if you wanted to be sure to have a hut all your own. I had just arrived and had opened up the beach chair provided by the hotel when a woman came puffing up and told me that I had to leave, it was her hut.

I was shocked. I was about to say, "Oh, I'm sorry," and fold up my chair again but something snapped inside. What was I doing? *I* was a person. I was there first. I had my rights.

"I'm sorry," I said. "I was here first and this is my hut."

"I was here first. It's not my fault I can't walk as fast as you. You saw me coming."

"Oh, no," I said, "I didn't see anyone. I was just looking at the water." I looked around for another vacant hut but they were all taken.

She stood glaring at me. I felt a little frightened but I knew I didn't have to be. I was in the right. Harold was always saying that I had to learn to solve problems as they came along. I looked at the angry woman. "Can we share this?" I asked. "You can have that side and my husband and I will take this side."

She drew herself up haughtily. "I do not share."

"I'm sorry," I said, "I do share." I opened my book, sat down, and started to read—or pretended to.

It seemed that she could finally share, after all. I pretended not to notice when she opened her beach chair and sulkily plopped down in it. Harold arrived and, thinking I had a new friend, started to talk to her. But she cut him off, pretending she couldn't see or hear him. He looked at me and I put my finger to my lips.

Well! I was not going to take this insult to my man on our second honeymoon. I stood up and turned my chair so that my toes faced her and I sat looking over my book, staring straight at her. I had discovered something. The joy of battle. The joy of holding your own.

"I don't know what you're doing, babe," Harold said softly, "but I never get involved in women's fights."

"Why not?"

"Because you can get caught in a lot of sniping and crossfire." He kept his back to us and worked calmly on his crossword puzzle, just as if we were on our patio in Cherry Hill. All morning long we were a silent hostile camp, this little ménage à trois. Harold and I took turns swimming so that one of us would be protecting our camp at all times . . . with the enemy and *her* several friends always leaving one behind to protect *their* camp.

I told myself it was not just a matter of justice and standing up for my rights—a person could get sunstroke without shelter from the tropical sun.

My greatest challenge came at lunchtime. Would I have to eat alone so that Hal could protect our territory? He still didn't know what was going on, so I had to figure it out myself . . .

My eye fell on the beachboy and suddenly I knew what to do. I walked over to him, pointed to our chairs, and said, "It is very important that those two chairs be exactly where they are now and that nobody move them." I showed him a five-dollar bill. "Do you think you would have time to watch them while we go to lunch?"

"No problem, ma'am," he said, tucking the bill into his colorful shorts.

At lunch I told Harold all about my little duel. Laughing, he took my hand across the table. "Beverly, what have we here? A tiger. I think you have graduated into the ranks of bitchy ladies. I don't have to protect you anymore. But God help me, who's going to protect me?"

I started giggling.

"Now what?" he said.

I told him that I would have known if my chair had been moved even an inch—I'd marked the spot where the back leg was!

He laughed again.

"I can't believe this is the same girl I brought home from the hospital. You've come a long way, baby."

As we packed early the next morning, I thought of my old nemesis and wondered if she'd be happy that the hut was all hers today. But I didn't really care. I was happy. At last, I was here. I had made it. I was grown-up. I was a fighter and Harold had a new respect for me. I could see it. Feel it.

"Are you ready, pal? I want to get to the airport early and we have to catch the hotel's six o'clock shuttle if we want to relax and catch the duty-free shops at the airport."

I was hardly listening to him because I had fastened onto one word, "pal." He had called me *pal*. That's what he called his buddies . . . *I* was his buddy. His friend. He was stalking ahead of me, no longer treating me like a helpless baby. Pals could take care of themselves.

We arrived at the airport so early that nothing was open—not even the coffee shop. Harold wandered around while I sat and watched the people. A well-dressed couple sat down next to me.

The man put out his hand. "Hello. I'm Hugh Carter."

And that's how it all began.

After Harold explained about my amnesia, Senator Carter said, "Thank God, I thought I was losing my mind! Oh, I'm sorry, I don't mean to sound unsympathetic."

He probed for details, then said I should write a book about it.

"Someone did write a story about me," I said, and told him about the *Ladies' Home Journal* piece.

"No. I'm talking about a book. You tell your own story. They'll never believe it. It's almost unbelievable. It really should be told. I'm going to give you the name of my collaborator and you call her and tell her what I said. She helped me with my memoir on the Carter family, *Cousin Beedie and Cousin Hot*. Jimmy was 'Cousin Hot'!"

The name was Frances Spatz Leighton and she lived in Washington, D.C. "She'll know what to do with it," he said. "You let me know how you make out."

"Oh, yeah," said Harold cynically, "we'll send you the first copy hot off the presses."

"Now hold on there," said Senator Carter, "stranger things than that have happened—like a peanut farmer from Plains becoming president."

We talked a long time and I was stimulated by the senator's questions. By the time we parted, I was no longer sad that the vacation was over—I could hardly wait to get home to start my book.

■ ■ ■

It wasn't so easy lining up my coauthor. Yes, she was pleased I had phoned her, and happy to hear about her good friend, Hugh Carter, but she was just now finishing up another project. And besides, she needed to feel that this book would be special.

And so began our long correspondence. Finally she agreed to come visit me and size up my family, my medical reports, my adventures. Some said, "Why don't you get another writer?" but I just had a feeling this was the one.

"No," I said. "She'll do it. You'll see. I'm going with what Senator Carter said."

Meanwhile, I turned back to my reality—life with Harold.

For a while he was happy in his new job as a salesman with a home remodeling company. But within weeks he was unhappy again. The company, he said, was holding back his commissions. "They want me to wait until the final payment but that isn't fair. I can't wait until they get their last penny. I've sold these accounts and I need my money."

After four months he left, still not having received a single payment. He went to work for another home remodeling company and started to make money, but he still wasn't happy. He didn't like their business practices—he felt guilty charging customers their exorbitant prices.

Again I heard, "It's not fair. It's not fair. I can't take advantage of people. I know what I should be charging, and I feel like a rat. I'd rather earn less and be able to live with myself. I'm not even proud of the job they do. The workmanship. People get taken."

"Why don't you tell the people so they won't be taken?"

"Then there would be all kinds of trouble and I wouldn't be bringing home these nice commission checks, would I? I'm concerned, but I'm not *crazy*."

"What do you mean?"

"I mean I'd be crazy to cut off my own neck, wouldn't I? Or, as you used to tell the children when they wanted to do something nasty to get even with somebody, 'Don't cut off your nose to spite your face.' "

"I said that?"

"You sure did."

I wrote it down. When I figured out what it meant, I decided I had been very wise.

"Well, you can't take full credit," Harold said. "You didn't make it up, you know. It's an old saying. Someone else said it long, long ago."

"Don't say *me. I* didn't say it. *She* said it."

"I know. The other Beverly. The Other Image."

Eventually Hal quit the remodeling company. He said that sometimes one did have to cut off one's nose to spite one's face after all. And he *said* he was relieved. But he sure didn't look it.

Now he called himself a free-lancer and he started working for many companies, getting contracts for remodeling jobs and turning them over to various companies that had the time and equipment to do them.

When he was home he was on the phone constantly, checking work on old contracts, lining up new ones. Once I asked if I could go along with him on a job estimate.

"Never," he said. "Never, never. Put that thought right out of your mind. I don't go along with you on your jobs, and you don't go along with me on mine."

"Why?"

"It's not a picnic. It's work."

He didn't know it, but I did rather imagine his work to be sort of a picnic. From what I'd heard, couples served coffee and cake or crunchy cookies and sat around talking about how to make their houses prettier. I was dying to see what everyone's house looked like. I would have been perfectly happy going up and down every street, knocking on doors, and saying, "May I see the inside of your house?" Fortunately I didn't think of it at the time or I *would* have done just that.

In June of 1983, Hal came home with a big smile on his face. Quite by chance he had met a manufacturer's representative who was opening up a new office for home improvements in the area. "This may be the break I've been waiting for," he said. "Something I can grow with and stick to until my retirement."

"What would you do?" I asked.

"The same thing. I'd be the sales rep, getting contracts to install the windows and siding they manufacture. This is top quality stuff. They manufacture some of the best products on the market. And they have only fine craftsmen for installers. I could be proud of every job I sold."

"But I don't see what's different from what you're doing now. You'll still be a salesman, won't you?"

"Right. But I wouldn't have to run around finding the company to do the work, free-lancing. I'd have a big company behind me—a good company."

"Yes," I said, but I still was puzzled by the way he seemed to change his tune with every job.

"Oh, honey, I forgot the most important thing—the opportunity for growth. Advancement. If things go well, I would become the manager of this office while the man I met went on to another city to open another branch. See?"

"I see. But I didn't know you wanted to be a manager."

"Well, I'm fifty-two. How much longer can I run around like this? I'd like a chance to handle an office and stay behind the scenes while younger men chase around."

"I'm happy for you," I said. Actually, I couldn't have disagreed more—but I knew it was the tactful thing to say. I was fifty-two also, and I had no intention of slowing down. I would have liked nothing better than to keep running faster and faster. But I knew what Hal would say to that . . . "You have all this energy because you're now only *three*—or *four* years old."

Several days later, I answered an ad in the paper for a job at a personnel company that referred doctors and medical technicians to hospitals and pharmaceutical companies. The owner was not a doctor, but her partner was.

There would be no salary, only commissions. They were looking for someone who understood medical jargon, could handle phone interviews, and be enough of a salesman to convince a candidate to switch jobs or go from medical school directly to the research lab or hospital.

"I'd like to try it," I told the owner.

I felt rather proud as I told Harold that I, too, would now be working on commission. He raised an eyebrow. "We shall see," he said. "We shall see."

In no time at all, I realized how hard it was to earn a commission. Appointments fell through. Doctors I was trying to interest in a particular job were initially enthusiastic and then abruptly changed their minds. I complained bitterly to Hal.

"Aha!" he said. "Now you understand. It only sounds easy."

Actually there were two parts to my job. First I had to call hospitals and research centers all over the country and find out if they were looking for doctors and if so, what type of doctor. Then I called medical schools to find out if anyone in their senior class was interested.

When very little happened to "put a jingle in my pocket book," as Shirley called it, I tried a new trick. I would call a hospital and ask for the resident doctors specializing in the area I was investigating. I would ask them if he would consider working for my client after their residencies were over. Sometimes they would say, "I've just begun my residency," and I'd feel rather foolish, but sometimes they were very interested—if not for themselves, then for a colleague who was dissatisfied in his or her present position.

I was thrilled whenever I completed a job swap—but thrills were about all I got. By the time I'd decided to quit, at the end of the summer, I figured out that I had averaged only about $200 a month—less than I made in a week of teaching for CETA and much more nerve-wracking.

Now I had a lot more respect for Hal and his work.

And so it was back to the want ads.

Again I saw the magic words—medical person, this time involving insurance. After hearing my qualifications over the phone, they invited me to come down and apply. Again, I didn't feel guilty about borrowing the qualifications of the Other Image, adding my own three jobs.

I was intrigued by the prospect of meeting all kinds of people in high places, going into their homes or places of business, seeing how they lived and worked. And I was determined to win their respect and admiration.

Unfortunately fear—not admiration—was all too often the reaction of my patients.

It was September, 1983. *My* month for new beginnings.

"Hello," I would say as I met the person who claimed to be too busy to go to the doctor's office for an insurance physical. "I'm Mrs. Slater. I'm a paramed for the Such-and-Such Insurance Company. I need to do a physical on you regarding the insurance you just purchased. Also, I'll need your medical history."

Then right there in the private office, I would take the individual's blood pressure, pulse, and urine specimen. No third person could be in the room during the examination—no secretaries, no bosses—probably on the theory that such persons could raise one's blood pressure.

When the applicant had given me his or her urine specimen, I would give it a quick tape test for obvious signs of diabetes, record my findings on the insurance form, and take the specimen to send to the lab for further testing.

Once a busy company president did not take the vial to his private bathroom but immediately unzipped his pants right in front of me—without even turning his back! My first impulse was to let the old Bev cuss at him and point him toward his private john, but . . .

"Tact, tact," I told myself as I turned my own back. What a glamorous job!

One day I got a phone call from a doctor who said that she, too, gave insurance physicals as a paramedic and had heard that I was good and reliable.

"That's nice," I said, wondering what my reliability had to do with her.

"The reason I'm calling," she continued, "is that I have to leave the New Jersey area and I promised my company to find someone very good and very dependable to take my place. Do you think you could handle the work for an additional insurance company?"

"Oh, yes," I said, "I have considerable time to spare. I'll just have to give up spending so many hours in art galleries and libraries."

We both laughed. "And probably churches," she added.

"A few," I said, "I have gone church-hopping. There are some great stained glass windows around here."

Soon I was earning as much as I had earned as a teacher and proving to her company how reliable a determined woman could be. One case involved an important trial lawyer who was always in court. I could never get him in his office. He was here. He was there. Mostly he was in court. If he *was* in his office, he was with a client and could not be disturbed.

But the insurance company was getting disturbed. I called the lawyer's secretary for the umpteenth time and as usual, he was in court. I hung up, waited, and called back, this time using a different voice. I said I was the clerk at City Hall and wanted to know in which courtroom the lawyer was trying his case that day.

She told me. Grabbing my equipment, I was out the door in a flash. I found my way to the room and listened to three cases disposed of or rescheduled until, finally, my lawyer stood up and began his presentation.

He won the case. He was standing and talking with the judge when I walked up to him, put out my hand and congratulated him. Then I said, "I'm Beverly Slater, a paramed for your insurance company, and I'm trying to do a physical on you."

He looked stunned. Before he could say anything I added with authority, "I'd like fifteen minutes of your time in the men's room." He and the judge stared at each other. "Please don't turn me down," I said quickly, "I've come quite a distance to see you."

Without a word, he shook his head and started gathering up his papers. The judge, laughing, said in mock alarm, "What's happening?" I laughed, too.

"Judge," I said, "I'm doing a physical for this man for his insurance policy, but if you need your blood pressure checked after all those cases you've heard, just meet us in the men's room."

He laughed again, even more heartily. The lawyer, still shaking his head, started out of the courtroom and I followed close behind. I still wasn't sure he was going to go along with this. But as soon as we were out of the courtroom, he turned and said, "I suppose you have the restroom picked out, too."

"No, I don't." I ignored his sarcasm. *(Tact. Tact.)* "I'll follow you."

He took me to the men's room of his choice and locked the door—which may have been the reason for his choice. Hardly a word was spoken as I took his blood pressure and pulse, and measured his chest. When I handed him the vial for the urine specimen, he snatched it from me, went into a stall, clanged the lock, and went about his business.

For a man who earned his living with words, he was strangely silent throughout the examination. At last, as he and I rose from the floor-administered EKG, he found his tongue.

"This is one for the legal books. I think you've just made the *Guinness Book of Records*, as well."

I laughed and proceeded to take his medical history, using the towel holder as my desk.

This wasn't the first time I'd administered an EKG in an unorthodox setting. Many an important man found himself lying across his desk or conference table as I dabbed on the electrode jelly and applied the terminals that would pick up the pattern of his heartbeats. If the desk was too small, I'd simply ask the individual to lie down on the carpet, and I would kneel beside him or her. Fortunately, I always wore a pants suit.

Once a decorator had no desk, no suitable carpeting. She ended up having her EKG on the ledge of a huge fountain in her showroom.

I loved my new job. I was paid by the number of examinations, instead of by salary, but at least I didn't have to wait for results— whether the individual got the insurance or not, I received *my* money almost immediately. It was like commissions, only better. No dry runs, no salesmanship. Every visit was paid for. But the best part was the adventure of meeting new people and peeping into their lives. I was learning by leaps and bounds everything that the old Beverly had known.

I often had to stop myself from becoming personally involved. Especially when I was taking medical histories, I would often feel the urge to interrupt with "Oh, I was at that hospital, too," or "I know your doctor," or "I know exactly how you feel because of what happened to me." But of course, I didn't.

One day I was scheduled to give an examination to a man in a wheelchair. I was already feeling a little down and the prospect didn't exactly thrill me. But I found myself telling him about being a victim of life myself, an amnesia victim, and before I knew it he had convinced me that he and I were the luckiest people in the world. We had survived! We could do anything! Nothing more could frighten us.

"What do you really want to do?" he asked.

"I guess write a book and tell people what it's really like to lose your memory. And find others like myself."

"What's stopping you?"

"Nothing."

I confessed that I was already working on my book, but that I still felt so lonely now and then that I wondered whether I just should have been left to die.

"Did you ever stop to think," my new friend said, "that you were spared in order to be an example for other people and help them go on?"

Of course. That *had* to be it. I did have a purpose. A mission. It *was* possible to come back from death, to start with a mind wiped almost clean of all knowledge and build a life again. *That* was a message worth living for. Worth talking about.

"Mrs. Slater continued to state how alone she felt because she was so different from everyone else. She talked about the publicity which she had sought regarding her amnesia, that she wanted to use it to help as many people as possible. She discussed her relationship with her family, stating that she could understand how she must have felt close to them before the accident because she found that she now liked them very much."

VII

REACHING OUT

18

Hospital Revisited

*I*n preparation for Frances Spatz Leighton's visit, Harold and I had gone over the description of amnesia that had appeared in the *Ladies' Home Journal* article.

"Part of your amnesia must be functional or hysterical," Harold said.

"Why?" I asked. "What makes you say that?"

"Because your symptoms vary from the standard amnesiac. According to Dr. Marcel Kinsbourne of Harvard Medical School, an amnesiac cannot remember what happened to her but she still has her skills—she knows how to do things."

"Well, I did know how to do things—like read and write." I was quite annoyed.

"Yes, but you couldn't do other things. You had to learn to eat with a fork and not your hands and needed help with getting dressed."

"Well, so what?"

"So it means you just might have lost some of your memory for emotional reasons—emotional trauma—along with your blanking out on your whole life story."

"Well, that's fine. So where does that leave me?"

"Beats me. Maybe you're going to remember suddenly all kinds of things you learned in school and not have to study them over again."

Together, Harold and I went over Dr. Kinsbourne's explanation of amnesia. He compared it to an electrical system in a house going on the blink. In the brain, the electric system is called the *limbic system.* If the circuitry breaks down, as in the case of a head injury, the message can't get through, and you have amnesia.

But had my limbic system been *permanently* damaged? According to Dr. Kinsbourne—and I'd heard this before—if certain parts of the brain are destroyed, that's it, and the mechanism that triggers memory cannot be recovered. So depending on the damage and cause of amnesia, the loss of memory could last a short time, many years . . . or a lifetime.

"Here's something very important . . . " I said. "Dr. Kinsbourne says there is no special part of the brain that is the storage place for what we know or experience. Every time something happens to us a new pattern is established. Then if something similar happens, it serves as a cue to the brain and we might react the same way we did before. We act on *cue.*"

"So what happened to you is you've lost your p's and q's."

"That's a bad pun. Forget it. I'm not talking to you."

Frances Spatz Leighton turned out to be a pussycat. We talked about why I wanted to write the book. I told her I wanted to communicate with others who had lost their memory. "I just want to know that I'm not alone."

I told her about my new friend Renée.

"This raises an interesting point," she said. "How many amnesiacs are out there? I'll try to find out."

Eventually she reported back that Public Health only kept statistics if there were at least 5,000 reported cases—evidently there weren't 5,000 amnesiacs in the United States. "You're in a very elite group," she said, laughing.

With each visit, Frances met more of my "cast of characters."

She could hardly wait to meet my doctors. First on her list was Dr. O'Connor.

After the passage of three years, I suddenly felt timid sitting in his waiting room—almost terrified. When he came out to meet me, I was so nervous I couldn't talk, but then he grabbed me and hugged me warmly.

So this was Dr. O'Connor, whom I had regarded with such awe—a combination God and father-figure—until I had transferred those feelings to Harold. How dignified he looked with his tall straight figure and iron-gray hair! "Did I curse at you the way I did my family?" I asked, sure he'd say no.

He laughed. "Of course. You didn't make exceptions. You displayed childish and uninhibited behavior—running away, cursing, and using foul language with everyone."

"What would you do when I talked like that?"

"We simply treated it as if we were speaking to a child. Waved it away with perhaps a 'Now, now,' or 'We know you don't mean that.' Or simply ignored it."

"The abusive language was only part of it," Dr. O'Connor continued. "At the hospital, her behavior was pretty uninhibited and at times violent. And she *was* like a child, ready to get out of the hospital and go home. I discharged her earlier than indicated simply because she was impossible to contain in the hospital without restraints and was constantly trying to escape. Her husband was permitted to take her home on his assurance that she would have a nurse."

"I did have a nurse," I said, "two nurses—until they taught me all about the kitchen and the house and how to take care of myself."

"Beverly was the greatest example of the inappropriate person," Dr. O'Connor said. "She could almost be counted on to say or do the inappropriate thing." He paused. "She was like a child."

"I know," I said. "Harold said I was like a baby who didn't know anything but could talk a blue streak—an articulate baby."

"How is Harold?" Dr. O'Connor asked. "Did he make out all right in business?"

"Oh, yes, he's doing fine now." Aha, so Harold *had* confided in the doctor about his business problems—and I hadn't even realized what was going on, let alone shown sympathy.

"Well, give him my regards. He certainly went through a lot with you."

Frances asked the doctor for his prognosis.

"Well," he said, "there was improvement in her childish behavior soon after she returned home and it continued steadily. We did not appreciate the full extent of the amnesia for some time. As far as amnesia goes, she is the only person I have ever had as a patient who had amnesia such as this—to such an extreme degree. We do not know the structural basis of the amnesia—why the brain is acting that way."

I held my breath, hoping he would continue. After pausing a

moment, he said "Mrs. Slater did sustain severe head injury and her life was at risk. She suffered cardiac and respiratory arrest, either once or twice, after the accident. A CAT scan showed there were changes evident both in the right parietal area of the brain and both frontal areas. Also, there was a fracture of the skull. But no surgery was necessary.

"Now as for her memory, it is impossible to predict if memory of her past life will ever return, but most surely her sense of taste and smell are permanently gone. I must admit, one concern is that the amnesia may be secondary to some kind of emotional or functional involvement. We don't know. It's a thought. It's an interesting case."

We went on to visit Dr. La Flare. Moments after we had him paged, he came striding off the elevators. How different he looked from the way I had remembered him!

I hadn't realized he was so tall. And there was a sprinkling of gray in his dark hair—had it been there before? I hadn't noticed. There was so much I hadn't noticed in my childlike hospital days—how handsome he was. I was almost shy as he greeted me warmly, taking my hand, then hugging me.

"So this is the real Beverly," he exclaimed. "You look lovely, all grown-up and in makeup."

I introduced him to Frances. She commented that it must be a nice feeling to see someone whose life one has saved and know how it all turned out. "It certainly is," he said. "Let's all have a cup of coffee and I'll tell you about Beverly—the Beverly I knew."

We walked to a large cheerful coffee shop adjoining the lobby and sat there for a long time, just talking.

"We—I mean the staff who took care of Beverly Slater—had a love-hate relationship with her," he said, "because we cared so deeply but she made it hard for us, fighting us every step of the way. She had come back from such a devastating injury that we of the inner staff looked at her recovery and eventual rehabilitation as a challenge.

"Once we were sure she was going to live, we were determined to make sure she would think and become a regular member of society. She had convulsions and all the symptoms that go with severe brain damage—the kind from which ninety-nine percent of the patients do not recover."

I could see how happy he was that I was functioning like everyone else—talking and smiling and drinking my coffee and understanding every word he said. "She made us emotionally involved, somehow. We *cared* what happened to her."

Frances asked about how *he* had handled me. "She could be difficult and she could be funny," he said. "When she cussed us out, we tried to ignore it because she was just being a naughty child. But sometimes we had to laugh because it was so unexpected and because she would let out a string of abuse so unlike the schoolteacher that she was—or had been."

I started to apologize, but he waved it aside.

"Most of the time she was a fun child, babbling along. She didn't need anyone to answer her, she just went merrily along. But of course, she changed moods rapidly. When she got the notion that she wanted to go home, she would take down her suitcase and throw some things into it. She would tell me, 'I've had enough. I'm packing.' "

"I don't even remember the suitcase," I said. "I don't remember packing. I don't remember telling you I was packing, that I'd had enough. But I remember Harold taking a suitcase home from the hospital because I had stolen restraints and hidden them in the suitcase and Harold was angry about that."

Dr. LaFlare laughed. "Oh yes, you did wreak havoc around there and you did spend a lot of time in restraints."

"But you're one of the lucky ones." He turned to Frances. "The greatest injury was to the occipital area in the back of the head. The spinal cord connects to the brain through the occipital area and I had to explain this to Harold. She had a basal fracture of the skull. Anything could be expected. It was a toss-up. Would she speak? Would she think? Would she walk? I believe it was ten or twelve days before her speech really made sense. Usually amnesiacs forget who they are but know the people around them. They may not know the names but they know that they know these people and have seen them before. Beverly could not remember seeing *anyone.*

"The more usual amnesiac may undergo some cataclysmic event that suddenly brings back his or her memory or it can be a simple thing. I recall one fellow who recognized where he lived and where to find his coffee jar and other things, but could not remember who lived there. Then a year or so later, he met a friend from childhood and in two hours things flooded back and he remembered everything and everyone."

"Does someone with amnesia automatically need a psychiatrist?" Frances asked. "Should every amnesiac seek psychiatric help?"

"Only if that person can't cope with life. It's not necessary to go to a psychiatrist unless one cannot cope with one's life."

I hated to say good-bye. Before we left Dr. LaFlare said, "As to Beverly's future, I'm not able to predict whether she will ever regain her memory. Given the severe brain damage, it is beyond the scope of medicine to predict. These things are hit-and-miss— it's unknown whether *anything* will return or how much she might regain.

"An event may take place years from now that will open the past and restore total memory of her life before the accident. But in such a case, whether this would wipe out the present is not known. That's really iffy." He chuckled. "Once in a while a blow on the head may cause return of memory—but that's the stuff of movies."

I left filled with many emotions. Maybe I would regain my memory—if I lived long enough. And if so, maybe I wouldn't even remember this wonderful experience of writing a book. Was I willing to lose the present to regain my past?

I didn't know. Did I have a choice? I didn't know.

If I'd had to choose at that moment, I think my answer would have been no thanks, I'll stick to the present.

19

Reaching Out

I knew I still needed help.

I had everything I wanted—a job I liked, a husband who was finally content with his career, friends and children who cared. I had even been flown to Jamaica, all expenses paid, as an honored guest.

So why couldn't I sleep at night? Why was I a victim—even prisoner—in my own apartment building, unable to get into an elevator? Why couldn't I have cocktails on the balcony with Harold and his friends? Why couldn't I stand to look down a mere ten stories? Why did I resent Other Image?

Why did I give in to Little Bev?

Could I retrieve my past? Did I want to?

Yes. I needed someone to talk to. I was finally ready to face the answers. I turned to my dear friend Bernice for the name of a psychotherapist.

"I guess I'm still afraid of therapy," I said. "It's as if I might slip back and have to go to a hospital again. I wish I could find someone like Dr. Veeder. But he's in Hartford, so that's impossible on a long-term basis."

"I know two men," Bernice said, "and I'm going to give you both their names but I'm going to tell you that the one I think you will feel best with is Dr. Elliot Atkins. He's a psychologist, and the thing you are going to like is his manner. He's young and relaxed and sort of casual and you won't feel intimidated." She told me that he was known for his work in drug rehabilitation and that he was very civic-minded. "And he is a local boy—he went to Temple."

"That's nice," I said. "But is he a *Mr.* or a *Dr.?*"

"You call him *Dr.* He got his doctorate at Temple. And this is something that will show you you can identify with him—he used to be an artist. A sculptor and painter. He got his bachelor's degree in fine arts. So you know he's not stiff and standoffish. But don't worry, under his casual air he cares a lot about his patients and he lets them know he cares."

"That's what I want. I'm getting along all right, but I can't sleep at night and I don't understand a lot of things and I need someone to understand or try to understand. I feel no one really understands. They want to but they can't. And they get bored if I keep telling them the same thing. If they gave me an answer, I would quit talking about it, but I don't have any answers."

"Well, I think Dr. Atkins would be relaxed and patient and maybe give you some answers. You know Bev, face it, only God knows all the answers. A psychiatrist or any kind of shrink is only the next best thing." She laughed.

But I was hurting too much to laugh. "Just give me the telephone number, Bernice. It's one thing I can't laugh about. And please, don't tell anybody what I'm doing. I don't even want Erma and Shirley to know until I feel better inside. If it doesn't work out, maybe I'll just never tell them, so don't you."

"That's your business, honey. I'll never tell them."

The instant I met Dr. Elliot Atkins, I felt that I had finally come *home.* He was smiling and cheerful. He even joked a little and made me laugh—about what I can't remember—but at least I wasn't scared anymore. Suddenly I felt in charge.

"I want to call you Elliot," I said immediately. "Is it all right with you? I don't like last names. Too cold."

He smiled. "That's fine. And I'll call you Bev. Is that all right?"

"That's fine. I like Bev better than Beverly."

Of course I wanted to know right away when he was going to give me *answers.* "My first job is to learn about Bev," he said, "and *you* are my best teacher. You will talk freely and say whatever is on your mind—anything, anything at all. And I'll have many questions. Then, maybe together, we'll find some answers."

I liked that. He wasn't playing the bigshot—he was doing what I had done at Camden Community College when I told the class I didn't know the answers but I would find them. I could trust him. We were going to have an adventure together and somewhere, together, we were going to find some answers.

"Elliot . . . can I ask a question?"

"Of course, Bev."

"When you do talk finally, I mean after I have talked and talked and told you all about my problems and all that—my amnesia and the things that are bothering me—then how much talking are you going to do? I mean, how much time out of my hour are *you* going to use to give me answers?"

"It isn't that way, Bev. No, I'm not going to sit here and lecture you. First you're going to do almost all the talking and then we're going to talk together. I doubt that I'll ever spend more than twenty percent of the hour doing the talking. Does that seem all right to you?"

"Oh that's fine. I just want to be sure you *will* talk. I mean not just a sentence or two. Okay, what do you want me to talk about?"

"Tell me about you. Tell me about Bev."

"Everybody says my son, Stuart, used to be my favorite," I said. "But now I don't even know if he likes me and I don't know how I feel about him . . ."

Why was I talking about Stuart? It had just slipped out. I guess it was bothering me. I just kept talking, trying to explain how I felt and why it mattered to me. Elliot was not looking at me. He was looking down, scribbling in a slim notebook with a nice leather cover. Before I knew it, the hour was up.

He smiled at me as he said good-bye and somehow I felt comforted, even though he hadn't told me what my attitude toward Stuart should be or said a word about what I should do. I was going to cooperate. I was going to work to make him understand me until he was ready to help *me* understand *myself*.

And I suddenly realized as I left Elliot's office that this was different from the times I had talked to Dr. Veeder. This time I wasn't starting out with what this person and that person had told me about the accident. This time I was talking about what *I* cared about.

I hadn't even *mentioned* the accident yet. And he hadn't asked. Maybe this was the right way—at least for me. Though he didn't talk, he seemed interested in me, encouraging me to go on and tell more. And I felt a warmth in him—Bernice was right.

I had to remember to thank her. Harold was always reminding me to thank people. That was very important to him. Along with tact, of course. I was going to have to figure out what was important to me and talk about it with Elliot.

But I knew what I didn't like: people lying to me or hiding things from me. How angry that made me when I found out later! Like when Harold had borrowed money from his father and let me believe that it was a bank loan, or when I found out that he had used all my insurance money and there was nothing left . . . Yes, I'd have to ask Elliot about that. How was I supposed to feel?

I told Elliot about my need to have everyone like me and approve of me. "A lot of people don't like my personality now and think I'm too forward, but I don't really care what they think about me. Maybe that's why I don't have high blood pressure anymore. I don't really care. It's possible. It could be."

He nodded his head and scratched on his pad. No answer.

There were two chairs in the room—one next to the desk and the other across the room—and I chose to sit in the chair next to the desk for two reasons. First I felt that he would understand me better if we looked each other in the eye, and I liked having a view out the window—looking at sky and trees soothed me when I was upset.

So every session I would sit in my chair next to the desk and ramble on about whatever was on my mind. At the beginning of every session, Elliot would just sit and wait for me to talk. Only in the last few minutes of a session would he say something like, "I have a question I'd like you to answer."

Rarely did he interrupt me.

I told him about how I was finding out that people weren't so wonderful and beautiful as I'd first thought when I came out of the hospital three years ago.

I told him about the different reactions I got when I approached strangers in restaurants and started talking to them, and one incident in particular, in which I had walked over to talk to a nice-looking man who, as it turned out, hadn't been friendly at all. He said, "Go back to your seat, miss, I don't *like* you." And I had just stood there paralyzed. I had gone back to Erma and Shirley's table in tears. When I told them what had happened, Erma had said, "Why are you so upset about it, Bev?"

"Because he didn't like me. Sometimes people don't like me."

"If they don't like you, it's their loss."

I felt so relieved—all this time I'd been feeling like a rejected child and suddenly it was all right. I didn't *have* to be liked by everyone. It was *their* loss!

Once when I was fretting about someone's problem, saying, "I can't solve it," Elliot asked, "Why do you take on other people's problems?" It gave me pause for thought. I *did* seem to spend a lot of time worrying about others . . .

"I know it's their problem," I said, "but I take it on as my problem. I feel I want to help. In the end I really feel it's my problem. It's confusing."

Elliot asked me about my friends. The words just poured from me as I talked about Erma, how I could not understand her, how I wanted to be like her and couldn't, how I had never heard her say anything bad about anybody. She was always saying you have to try to understand *why* someone did something. And whenever something bad happened, she would say, "Wait. Something good will come of it. Something good always comes out of bad." When I asked what was good about what happened to *me*, she said, "*You* like yourself more now. You seem to be enjoying yourself more. You're not worrying about all the things that can go wrong."

"I guess I'm not worrying because I don't know all the things that can go wrong," I told Elliot. "I'm a dummy." And I started to cry. "I'm so afraid Harold will think I'm a dummy. I'm trying so hard but I still feel like a dummy when people are talking about things and I don't know what they're talking about and they have to explain—like about World War II and "M*A*S*H." Hal watches everything about war. I go into the other room. I don't watch anything about war or prisons. I can't stand people in boxes. I can't stand being closed in. I feel something's tightening around my heart and I have to get away. I like windows. I'm glad you have windows. In intensive care there was a big window, only it wasn't to see the outside. It was facing the nurses' station and when I was better I would watch the nurses through my big window and then later, when I was walking around I saw the other kind of window looking outside at the world and the people. And I was so

amazed to see buildings outside and one building had some
words on it and I thought it was beautiful. And three years later
when I went back with Frances, I saw the same street and I
showed her what I had looked at from the hospital window and it
was ugly and old and just some small ugly building around the
hospital and the name on the building was in old, old lettering,
maybe a hundred years old and told the name of the man who had
his business there. But at least I learned about windows from
these buildings. And now I know people are the same. They have
windows and they can look out and they have other windows and
they can look in deep inside."

I was still crying. "It's hard to look inside. I don't know what I'm
looking for."

I told Elliot that I felt ashamed I still wasn't part of the world.
After all this time, I said, it still seemed as though I was on the
outside looking in, watching people so that I could learn how to
behave.

I told Elliot so much. I cried a lot. I said I was still scared about
therapy—about finding out things about myself. I told him about
my "pretend" psychiatrist. I wanted my family to think I was
doing what was right. Especially Stuart. I talked about Stuart the
most. I don't know why it was so important to make *him* think I
was going. Why I cared most about what *he* thought. I still don't
know . . .

I asked Elliot what he thought about this: when Harold was
showing me how to drive the car, the first thing he said was,
"Where is the brake?" and I showed him. He told everyone about
this, saying he didn't know if that was residual memory or if I had
just been so good at watching him that I had picked it up. Elliot
just looked at me and gave a little shrug.

Harold didn't ask me what I talked about during my sessions,
but once he asked if it wasn't hard to find things to say for a whole
hour.

I had to laugh.

I talked to Elliot about Little Bev, and about how I'd learned to
keep the child inside me. Now whenever I was very sad or upset,
and she took over, saying, "Screw it," or, "I'm getting out of here. I
don't need this," I would tell her that maybe we'd better stay and
face it, whatever it was. She would go back down again, deep
inside. Sometimes, I confessed, I *preferred* Little Bev.

One day, toward the end of the session, Elliot asked me if I wanted to regain my memory.

I paused. "First I have another question. If I regain my memory, will I lose the memory of my last three years?"

He didn't answer that question. "If you had your choice, would you like both or would you like to give up your present memory?"

"I *know* myself now. You're asking me if I want to remember and know an image that's a stranger to me. I don't know her. I only know myself. So maybe I don't want to remember her because I don't *know* her. What I want is to remember *both*, or forget the past. I like myself today and I won't give myself up willingly."

At the end of every session he would ask questions like, "How do you feel about your children?" or "How do you feel about your mother and father?" or "How do you feel about your husband?"

I was always caught off guard by such questions, but I liked that. It felt good to get a lot of stuff out without worrying about whether the person I was talking to approved or disapproved of what I was saying.

Even though I often spent the better part of the hour crying, I would leave Elliot's office feeling that a little more of my load had been lifted. It was a wonderful feeling.

———————————

"Interestingly enough, the fact that she has given herself three years to live does not seem to worry her too much and I would suspect that, at some level in her consciousness, she either does not believe this or is hopeful that she may be wrong."

20

You Are Not Alone

*T*he next time I saw Frances she had done some homework on me. "You are not alone," she said, waving some papers at me. "Look. Other cases. You can read about other people who've had amnesia. It was a bitch getting anything like this at all. You really are in a very select group."

I read the first case. Amazing. But it wasn't like *me*. "This isn't my case at all," I said. "It's fascinating, but it's not me."

"Of course not," she said. "No two cases are alike. That's what makes it so fascinating. And so complicated for doctors to predict what will happen to the patient. They still don't understand fully the workings of the brain when it comes to normal memory, and many studies are going on. Even experts differ on how the memory works and how we retrieve or call back a tiny item of information from our brain when we want it. Is it neatly filed? Is it filed helter-skelter?"

"Are there books on it that I can read?"

"There are books, but so technical that I couldn't fully understand them. One that is supposed to be very good is by one of the outstanding experts on the subject of amnesia, Laird Cermak, a psychologist in Boston, at the Veterans Administration Medical Center. You know, military men sometimes suffer amnesia from head wounds and Dr. Cermak says certain alcoholics suffer permanent amnesia."

In retracing my steps and going over my old notes, Frances tracked down Dr. Cermak. On the phone he told her that most of the cases of amnesia he worked with were linked to alcoholism. Frances asked how long this type of amnesia lasted.

"It can be permanent," he said.

When she asked how many amnesiacs there were in the United States, Cermak said there was no way of knowing, but that it was a relatively rare phenomenon. In his twelve years of practice, he said, he had only had forty cases.

Frances and I went over the information she had gathered on other amnesia cases. There was a *McCall's* magazine article about a woman named Sarah who, after an operation for a stroke, awoke thinking that it was 1960, she was twenty-three years old and had three little toddlers, when in fact it was 1976, she was thirty-nine years old, and had four almost grown children!

The article, written by Joan Potter, entitled "Missing: Sixteen Years of My Life," tells how the amnesic woman, Sarah, first catches sight of her fourth child—whom she doesn't even remember having given birth to—when her husband brings her to the hospital. He introduces a tall girl with long brown hair to Sarah who, the article says, "just sat and looked at her. She had no idea who Kelly was." I know exactly how she felt.

But at least Sarah knew who *she* was. She knew who her husband was. And she knew some of the people of her past.

I was pleased to see that I had many things in common with Sarah. Just as I had forgotten how to do needlepoint, she had forgotten how to knit. Like me, she had trouble remembering what objects were called, and she had to write things down so that she could remember names of people and things she was supposed to do.

And most important, Sarah had undergone a personality change just like mine. According to some family members, before the operation she was an independent, aloof person, totally devoted to her husband and children. *Aloof* was the exact word Fayne had used to describe *me.* And the rest of the description could have been about me, as well. But now her mother-in-law said, " . . . when she comes in the house she hugs and kisses me."

Wasn't that exactly what my own family said? Joanie said that I never used to kiss her until after the accident. I cried when I read that. Tammy, Sarah's daughter, had said that now when her mother was in the bedroom sitting and knitting, she liked to go in and sit on the bed with her and talk.

Tammy said, "I tell her everything." Before her mother was "more restrained" and "busy playing the role of wife and mother." Tammy concluded, "I loved her through all her phases, but this one I like the best." It could have been Joanie talking.

Why did Sarah lose sixteen years? Why not five years or twenty? That's what Sarah and I wanted to know. Her doctor, neurosurgeon George Allen, says there is no answer to that yet.

Dr. Harold Goodglass, director of psychology research, Boston Veterans Administration Medical Center, is quoted in the *Mc-Call's* article as saying that no one knew exactly *what* had caused Sarah's amnesia. It could have been the tiny clips sealing off the blood vessels in the brain during the operation. It could have been the surgery itself. It could have been the original aneurysms in the wall of the artery in her brain, one of which had ruptured and caused a blood clot.

Dr. O'Connoer wasn't exactly sure what had caused my amnesia either. It could have been the strike of the head on the pavement. It could have been the backlash, the way the contents of the skull—the brain and nerves and blood vessels—were shaken back and forth from the force of the blow. It could have been the bleeding inside the head. It could have been the swelling.

I really felt close to Sarah, and was determined to find her after I'd finished with the book. Maybe her doctor would tell me how to reach her.

I was interested to see, too, that Sarah's writer had done her homework on amnesia theories and how memory works. "A memory loss does not mean that the missing memories were stored in the injured spot," Potter wrote. "The damage might have been to some connection or crossroad in the brain."

I was certain something was wrong with one of my crossroads or connections.

I could not believe the variety of amnesia cases written about in *Amnesia: Clinical, Psychological and Medicolegal Aspects*, a highly technical British book that was edited by two doctors and included thumbnail sketches of amnesiacs.

One case that fascinated me was that of a forty-five-year-old man who had been admitted to a hospital for "fits" and who told the doctors that fifteen years before, when he was thirty, he had awakened in a hospital with no memory of his identity or "any event of his previous life." He had been brought in with no identification.

So far, that was me. And as I recall, Dr. LaFlare and Dr. O'Connor said that I had had convulsions during those first few days at the hospital.

But the man was not as lucky as I; no one came forward to claim him. Eventually he was released and he had to give himself a name. He selected a name from the shop opposite the hospital— "James Williamson."

Like me, he was "able to relearn general information rapidly," and in two years he was holding a good job and earning a good salary as a foreman in an engineering company. He kept trying to trace his family and finally after three years he was reunited with a brother who told him he had a wife and three young children. And the amazing thing was his real name . . . it was "William Jameson."

I could hardly wait to see if he rushed to find his wife. No. He didn't even take back his real name. He continued living with his girl friend and didn't meet his wife until he went to see his mother after hearing that she was terminally ill. According to the case history, "At her deathbed the memory of his former life returned in full."

I was surprised to learn that sometimes the personality change resulting from a head injury is not for the better. In one case, a thirty-two-year-old theology student was about to start his career as a minister, when he suffered amnesia after a car accident. He lost only six months of memory, but his personality change was so radical that he was unable to continue in his chosen profession. He was "euphoric and inconsequential in conversation and could not maintain the thread of his talk for more than a few minutes."

Besides that, he would have sudden "inappropriate" outbursts of laughter or anger, or would cry. That was the very word my doctors had used about my behavior in the hospital—*inappropriate.* But I had eventually overcome it, and had even developed a modicum of tact. This poor man could not, and his friends considered him "mildly demented."

Again I realized how lucky I was.

I got a little laugh out of one case that had the doctors scratching their heads. A twenty-two-year-old motorcycle delivery man who was thought to have short-term amnesia (because he knew his army identification number from past service and even knew that he had been transferred to a second hospital) seemed unable to remember his correct age—he consistently subtracted two years. Finally they discovered that he was giving the details of another motor accident that had taken place two years before, and after which by strange coincidence he had been taken to a second hospital.

Both Drs. Whitty and Zangwill said that it was always a good idea to reassess amnesia in trauma patients like myself some time after they seem to be back on the track and remembering day-to-day events again. They said that often doctors mistakenly assume that the patient has fully recovered when his responses to questions involving short-term memory seem normal.

For example, he might answer yes, he remembers going to the x-ray department, but later he might not be able to recall anything about it. In other words, normal memory has not yet been reestablished. I know this was the case with me—frequently I couldn't remember the answers I had given someone or the questions they had asked, even though the person kept insisting I must know.

I learned also about a study made after World War II of seventy-four amnesia patients who experienced head injury or trauma, sudden loss of memory, and loss of personal identity. In thirty-six of the cases, the doctors involved were able to determine that the amnesia was indeed organic. In twenty-seven cases, psychogenesis was the major factor—"severe depressive or anxiety state"—and the trauma merely provided the occasion for "a motivated functional amnesia." In only five cases did the patients confess that they were assuming the trappings of amnesia to malinger and shirk their duty. The other seven cases, it seems, involved various degrees and combinations of organic and psychogenic conditions.

There was also a study on the effectiveness of the "twilight state," the sleepy, uninhibited condition induced by hypnosis or drugs such as pentothal used in the treatment of amnesia. Research doctors found this condition to be more effective in organic amnesia than in the purely psychogenic type. But the results, in general, were disappointing. Of forty cases, only twelve had a lasting reduction of amnesia after their "sleep."

Here was an exciting thought—maybe *I* would be one of the lucky ones who remembered. But it was scary, too. I liked my new me better than the Other Image . . . but there was certainly an inducement to see a hypnotist—especially when I read about a military man who after a car accident (he regained consciousness in minutes) had lost all knowledge of who he was, his past, and even simple motor skills. In the next six months he relearned all his technical skills very rapidly—just as I did—and retained the knowledge of whatever was told him about his previous life, but he still had no recollections of his own.

Then "suggestion under amylobarbitone narcosis" was tried, and he remembered everything of the past, even when he woke up. But one question was not answered in the sketch—after his "sleep" did he return to his "old" self or did he remain the new person he had become?

Eventually, while we were still finishing the book, Frances brought an article from the Fairfax, Virginia *Journal* about an amnesia case that was even worse than mine. Entitled, "Life After a Head Injury," the article told about a girl named Barbara Whitlock, of Rockville, Maryland, who had been in a coma for a month after an auto accident and who virtually came out of it like a newborn baby. According to her parents, she had no memory at all of her life before the accident. Her father is quoted as saying, "She had to learn to walk, talk, be toilet trained." At least I could walk. And I could talk, even though it was gibberish at first. And even though I didn't know what a toilet was, I didn't have to be toilet trained.

There is a happy ending to Barbara's story, just as there is a happy ending to mine. She is now going to college, even though, as her father says, "We were told she would never be a useful citizen again."

The secret of our rehabilitation is of course studying. Books, books, and more books. I don't know if Barbara did it exactly the way I did, but according to the article, her mother, Beverly, spent more time helping her daughter study than she did in her own job.

The article states that Barbara, like me, still has trouble remembering things. Very often I find myself confused about certain events surrounding the accident, even though I have been told them repeatedly.

As a result of her daughter's experience, Beverly Whitlock has started the Maryland Head Injury Foundation, whose goal is to improve the quality of life for people who have suffered brain injuries. I have saved Beverly's name and address because someday I, too, might like to start such an organization. Perhaps *that* is my destiny. I feel uplifted, inspired just learning what one woman can do to help not only one person but others, too.

Harold laughed when I told him. "This could be a turning point. Be sure to tell your friend Elliot next time."

"I will," I said. "I will. And I'm really starting to feel better somehow. I don't know how to explain it, but I really want to live now. And I don't think it's just because I'm writing the book. Maybe that number three that's always hanging over my head isn't going to fall on me. It's not so ominous."

"Of course it's not going to fall on you. You know, *I* have an inspiration, too. Have I told you what *I* feel the number three means?"

"I don't know," I said. "I don't think so."

"Well, my inspiration tells me the three refers not to three *years* but to three *people.*"

I felt a sudden chill. "Are you making fun of me?"

"No, babe, no. I'm not making fun of you."

"Who are the people?" I demanded. "Who?"

"It's Joanie and Stuart and me, of course. We're the three reasons you had to live."

I had a strange feeling, as if a weight had been lifted off me. At once I was laughing and crying. "That would be too simple," I blubbered. "But great truths are simple, aren't they? I don't know. I don't know."

"But *I* know," he said, hugging me and dancing me around the room.

I reminded Harold about my feeling that I did not have long to live.

"Tell me, babe, what makes you persist in that idea even when you know the three years are up? It's more than three years since your accident. You're safe. So what's this all about?"

"I know I should feel safe, but I can't."

"Well, where did you get the idea you had three years?"

"From the number 3 I saw when I was dead. But I saw it two times and you said I was dead two separate times. Now I'm thinking I've used up my first three years and I'm working on the second, so I have to hurry."

"Well, I can't fight your fantasies but I think you're going to live a long time and you'd better let a professional get this dumb idea out of your mind."

I laughed. "You can say *dumb* and it doesn't bother me. Everybody's dumb in some way. Even smart people are dumb in a lot of things." Then I started to cry. "I guess the word *dumb* does still hurt a little, after all."

Harold held my head on his shoulder. "You're still a little mixed up, kiddo. You still need a little help."

"And I'm getting it, you dummy," I shot back. "What do you think Dr. Atkins is all about?"

Harold clapped his hand to his cheek. "I don't believe it. The lady called me a dummy."

I broke away, giving him a triumphant look. "I guess I could live with that. I've lived with *you*, haven't I?"

Now we were both laughing. "Beverly," exclaimed Harold, "what's happening to you? You're developing a sense of humor!"

Statement of Dr. Elliot L. Atkins, Beverly Slater's current psychologist:

Concerning Beverly, there was organic damage to her brain that has been documented. There was a personality change. There was amnesia following the head trauma, which continues on today.

Whether, on her own, she can or will regain memory appears to be unlikely. However, with psychotherapy, there is a chance for her, though it is an uphill battle.

Some therapists feel that hypnosis or the use of drugs to bring back a sudden rush of memory is a useful clinical tool with amnesiacs. My concern in Beverly's case is that the amnesia is serving to protect her from unacceptable emotions and we have to be careful how we reconnect her with her memory. Total amnesia is extremely rare. It is safe to say in this case, part is emotional or psychogenic in nature.

Beverly and her family have made a commitment to continue this exploration process. It is hoped that in this way, in time, the conditions would be forthcoming, that would allow Beverly to require the amnesia no longer.

"... *There is no question but that the trauma that Mrs. Slater suffered has affected her considerably ... I feel certain that the childlike extroverted quality which she exhibits, together with the marked emotional lability (she would laugh and cry accompanied by the appropriate emotional response within very short periods of time) is indicative of frontal lobe pathology. Where the functioning of the frontal lobes is compromised, one tends to see changes in personality in which judgment, particularly social judgment, can be impaired and the emotional response can be affected. Where there is severe compromise of frontal lobe functioning, one might see dullness and apathy. However, in less severe frontal lobe impairment, one not infrequently sees the kind of emotional lability which I have described in Mrs. Slater.*

"*Although her social judgment does appear to be impaired, nevertheless, it is not severely so and, by her own account, she appears to be learning to curb her tactless comments to people such as criticizing clothes that they might wear or the colors that they choose, and she is attempting to be less forward in approaching strangers.*

"*The complicating factor comes about when one attempts to evaluate her amnesia. I feel quite certain that, although one would expect some memory impairment as a result of the head trauma she suffered, the total amnesia which she claims does seem to me to be of psychogenic origin. I do believe that Mrs. Slater demonstrates hysterical defense mechanisms which, I suspect, were a part of her personality prior to the accident. Her husband told me that although she was not as outgoing as she is now, nevertheless, she was always a lively person, was considered to be a good teacher, and had qualities which enabled her to identify closely with people with whom she came into contact ...*

"*The waters are further muddied by virtue of the fact that, in the hospital and when she returned home, she was never really given the opportunity to learn for herself. Everybody appears to have responded to her 'needs' by pointing things out to her, 'jogging her memory' and, I suspect, after a time not expecting her to remember anything. It was apparent to me in our conversations that the amnesia was not as total as every-*

one, including Mrs. Slater, believed. There were things that she remembered and which she does not recall as having been told . . .

"However, it is extremely important to remember that hysterical amnesia is a very real syndrome, and that although there appears to be some obvious contradictions in what Mrs. Slater says she can remember and what she cannot remember, this condition is not under her conscious control, however obvious the contradictions may seem to the observer. I have witnessed people with hysterical blindness who were quite certain that they could not see but who, nevertheless, avoided bumping into objects and never hurt themselves because of their 'lack of sight.'

"I think we are dealing with a mixed picture in which both organicity and hysteria are interwoven."

A Final Note

Who am I?

I'm afraid to find out.

The new Beverly loves playing craps at the casino. The old Beverly had to be coaxed into spending a few nickles and dimes on the one-armed bandits. The new Bev says whatever is on her mind, no matter how outrageous. The old Beverly was conservative and measured her words. The old Beverly took medication for high blood pressure. The new Bev doesn't need any.

To the new Bev, there are no strangers.

My friend Bernice says, "Bev, you were a good friend in the old days but you were dull, dull, dull! I have to tell you, dear. Don't ever go back, even if you have to find someone to hit you over the head again to forget the past. I vote for the new Bev!"

So do I.